An Irish Almanac ✓

An Irish Almanac

Aidan H. Crealey

MERCIER PRESS

Mercier Press Ltd
PO Box 5, 5 French Church Street, Cork, Ireland

and
24 Lower Abbey Street, Dublin 1, Ireland

© Aidan H. Crealey, 1993

ISBN 1 85635 035 5

First published 1993
10 9 8 7 6 5 4 3 2 1
A CIP catalogue record for this book
is available from the British Library.

For Ruairi, Diarmuid, Deirdre and Elizabeth

Printed in Ireland by Colour Books Ltd.

Contents

Introduction

An Irish Almanac presents Irish history – political, social, economic and cultural – on an 'On this Day' basis, along with a comprehensive list of forthcoming centenaries (1994–2003). The reader can check at a glance the major anniversaries for any particular day of the year. The extensive index provides easy access to information on notable persons and events.

Included here is information and commentary on notable personalities and events in Irish political history from the Battle of Clontarf (April 1014) to the Maastricht Referendum of June 1992, as well as extensive coverage of other aspects of Irish society, including literature and scholarship, music and the arts, clerical and criminal matters and the Irish abroad. Over seventy million people in the world claim Irish descent

An Irish Almanac is the ideal companion for the armchair historian, quiz-master, tourist, raconteur, student, speechmaker or indeed for anyone interested in the rich and varied world of Irish history.

January

1801: Act of Union, uniting parliaments of Great Britain and Ireland, became law.

1891: Patrick MacGill, author, notably of *Children of the Dead End* (1914), born in Glenties, Co. Donegal, the first of eleven children of a small farmer.

1926: 2RN broadcasting station, later Radio Éireann and RTE Radio One, officially opened by Douglas Hyde.

1973: Ireland joined European Economic Community (EEC) along with Denmark and United Kingdom.

1905: First edition of *Irish Independent*.
    Owned and edited by William Martin Murphy, was result of merger between Murphy's *Daily Nation* and *Irish Daily Independent*, founded by Charles Stewart Parnell. Companion paper, the *Sunday Independent* began publication a year later.

1905: Padraic Fallon, poet and playwright, author of verse play *Diarmuid and Grainne* (1950), born at Athenry, Co. Galway.

1946: William Joyce, 'Lord Haw-Haw', Nazi propagandist who

spent much of youth in Galway, hanged in Wandsworth jail
for treason.

4/1

1961: Death of character actor Barry Fitzgerald, stage name of
William Joseph Shields.

1969: 'Burntollet Ambush' in Northern Ireland.
People's Democracy marchers, on trek from Belfast to
Derry, ambushed by Loyalist mob at Burntollet Bridge near
Claudy, Co. Derry. Approximately three hundred injured.

5/1

1922: Sudden death on the island of South Georgia in the South
Atlantic of Sir Ernest Shackleton, Antarctic explorer.

1953: Twenty-seven people killed when BEA Viking aircraft
crashed at Nutt's Corner, now Belfast airport.

1973: Death of Gerald Boland, founder member of Fianna Fáil and
minister in various Fianna Fáil governments.

1976: Death of John Aloysius Costello, barrister, politician and
Taoiseach in the first two coalition governments (1948–51
and 1954–7).

  : 'Kingsmills massacre' in Northern Ireland.
Eleven Protestant workmen taken at gunpoint from minibus at Kingsmills crossroads in South Armagh and gunned
down by the roadside. Only one survived.

6/1

1834: Death of Richard Martin, landlord.
Martin, whose estates in Connemara, Co. Galway comprised
200,000 acres, earned himself two sobriquets: 'Hair Trigger
Dick', on account of fondness for duelling, and 'Humanity
Martin' for generosity to his tenants. Founding member of
Royal Society for the Prevention of Cruelty to Animals (1824)
and grandfather of novelist, Mary Letitia Martin.

1839: The 'Night of the Big Wind'.

Hurricane force winds and heavy rain during night of 6–7 January caused more widespread damage than any storm in recent centuries. In Dublin area alone, some 5,000 houses had damage ranging from broken windows to complete destruction. On one Co. Mayo estate, storm felled over 70,000 trees.

1839: General Post Office, O'Connell Street, Dublin, opened to public.

Destroyed during 1916 Rising, GPO was designed by Francis Johnston.

1898: Colonel James C. Fitzmaurice, aviator and co-pilot on first Atlantic east–west flight (1928), born in Dublin.

7/1

1914: Death of Patrick Weston Joyce, historian and music-collector.

Joyce, from Glenosheen, Co. Limerick best remembered for his three-volumed *Origin and History of Irish Names of Places* (1869, 1875, 1913). Younger brother, and fellow scholar, Robert Dwyer Joyce, wrote a number of patriotic ballads including 'The Boys of Wexford'.

1922: Ratification by Dáil Éireann of Anglo-Irish Treaty of December 1921, by 64 votes to 57.

1965: Death of Jimmy O'Dea, comedian who dominated the Dublin music hall stage from 1920s to 1950s.

1975: Death of Sinéad De Valera (née Flanagan), wife of Eamon De Valera.

8/1

1871: James Craig, Lord Craigavon, Unionist leader and first Prime Minister of Northern Ireland (1921–40), born in Belfast.

1910: Marriage at St Paul's Church, Arran Quay, Dublin, of Eamon De Valera and Sinéad Flanagan, a teacher.

1941: Death of Frederick Robert Higgins, poet, author of the collection *The Gap of Brightness* (1940).

1979: Death of fifty people, of whom forty-three French citizens, when oil-tanker, *Betelgeuse*, exploded at Whiddy Island, Bantry Bay, Co. Cork.

1989: Death of forty-four people, mostly from Northern Ireland, when Boeing 737, on flight from London to Belfast, crashed at Kegworth in Leicestershire. Three of injured died later.

9/1

1594: Trinity College Dublin, Ireland's first university, opened its gates to students.

Trinity designed to wean Gaelic Irish away from continental European establishments such as Louvain. Abel Walsh was first student enrolled; James Ussher, later Church of Ireland Archbishop of Armagh, was second.

1642: Massacre at Island Magee, Co. Antrim.

Thirty Catholics slaughtered by Scottish garrison and English settlers from Carrickfergus, Co. Antrim.

1929: Brian Friel, playwright, born in Omagh, Co. Tyrone. Many plays include *Philadelphia Here I Come* (1964), *Translations* (1980) and *Dancing at Lughnasa* (1991).

1984: Death of Seán MacEntee, founder member of Fianna Fáil and former Tánaiste.

10/1

1941: Death of Sir John Lavery, leading Irish landscape and portrait painter.

In 1923, Lavery commissioned by Irish government to design new paper currency of Irish Free State. His portrait of his wife, Lady Lavery, as Cathleen Ní Houlihan subsequently appeared on all Irish banknotes. Lady Lavery's portrait has now become watermark.

1945: Death of twenty-three people in two-train collision at Bally-macarrett junction, Belfast.

11/1

1836: George Sigerson, physician, scientist and writer, notably of *The Bards of the Gael and Gall* (1897), born at Holly Hill, Strabane, Co. Tyrone.

1837: Death in Moscow of John Field, composer and pianist.
   Field, born in Dublin, wrote some 20 nocturnes, 7 concertos and 4 sonatas. Buried in Moscow's Vadensky cemetery where a monument fashioned out of fine green stone erected in his honour.

1972: Death of Padraic Colum, poet and dramatist. Plays include *The Land* (1905) and *Thomas Muskerry* (1910).

12/1

1729: Edmund Burke, orator and political philosopher, born in Dublin. Works include *The Sublime and Beautiful* (1757).

1885: Thomas Ashe, patriot, born in Kinard, Co. Kerry.

13/1

1800: Daniel O'Connell made his first public speech, at the Royal Exchange in Dublin, in protest against the Act of Union.

1941: Death in Zürich of James Joyce, poet, novelist and play-wright. Author of *Ulysses* and *Finnegans Wake*.

14/1

1753: Death of George Berkeley, metaphysical philosopher, theologian, educationalist and Bishop of Cloyne from 1734.

1965: Meeting between Taoiseach Seán Lemass and Northern

Ireland Prime Minister Captain Terence O'Neill, at Stormont, breaking the ice in cross-border relations for first time since partition.

15/1

1821: Thomas Clarke Luby, co-founder of Irish Republican Brotherhood (IRB) or Fenian movement (1858), born in Dublin, son of a Church of Ireland minister.

1861: Death in San Francisco of Terence Bellew MacManus, Young Irelander.

1988: Death of Seán MacBride, revolutionary, politician and first Irishman to be awarded Nobel and Lenin Peace Prizes.

16/1

1922: Dublin Castle, for centuries seat of English rule in Ireland formally handed over to Free State authorities by Lord Lieutenant, Lord Fitzalan.

1941: Outbreak of foot-and-mouth disease confirmed at Eglinton, Co. Derry.
    Disease soon spread across border to become worst recorded outbreak in history. By the time it was eradicated, in September 1941, over 40,000 animals had been slaughtered.

17/1

1861: Death of Lola Montez, stage-name of Eliza Gilbert, dancer.
    Born at Kilfinnane, Co. Limerick, became virtual ruler of Bavaria after performance in Munich in 1847 attracted attention of aging King Ludwig who made her his mistress. Banished after insurrection in 1848, she settled in America and gave lectures on gallantry, beautiful women and heroines of history. Devoted last years to care of the inmates of Magdalen Asylum, New York.

1862: Douglas Hyde, writer, scholar, translator and first President of Ireland (1937–45), born at Frenchpark, Co. Roscommon.

1866: Death of George Petrie, painter, musician, and antiquary.

1992: In Northern Ireland, seven Protestant workmen engaged in construction work with British army killed and six others seriously injured, when their minibus blown up by IRA near Teebane Crossroads, Co. Tyrone.

18/1

1893: Reginald Ingram Montgomery Hitchcock, sculptor, film director and writer, born in Rathmines, Dublin.
Hitchcock, who styled himself 'Rex Ingram' directed over 20 films including *The Four Horsemen of the Apocalypse* (1920).

1934: Death in his native Belfast of Joseph Devlin, affectionately known as 'Wee Joe', Nationalist MP at Stormont and MP at Westminster for Fermanagh and Tyrone.

1937: John Hume, co-founder of Northern Ireland's Social Democratic and Labour Party (SDLP), MP and MEP, born in Derry.

19/1

1785: Richard Crosbie ascended in a balloon from Ranelagh Gardens, Dublin, to become first Irish airman.

'... from the most certain account, we can inform the town that in about ten minutes after he became invisible on his ascent, he landed in perfect safety on the strand, near the Island of Clontarf.'

The Freeman's Journal

1787: Mary Aikenhead, founder of Irish Sisters of Charity and St Vincent's Hospital Dublin, born in Cork.

1802: Death of Francis Higgins, the 'Sham Squire'.
Born of poor parents who migrated from Downpatrick, Co. Down to Dublin, became known as 'Sham Squire' after he induced lady of means to marry him under guise of being landed gentleman. Served Crown as paid informer; little doubt that he was 'FH' recorded as receiving £1,000 for discovery of Lord Edward FitzGerald.

20/1

1902: Kevin Barry, first IRA Volunteer to be executed during Anglo-Irish War, born in Dublin.

1968: Death of Sir Alfred Chester Beatty, mining engineer, philanthropist, art collector, and first honorary citizen of Ireland.

Born in New York; began mining career as labourer on 25 cents an hour, graduating in 10 years to foreman, manager, mine-owner and millionaire. In 1950 settled in Ireland, where became known as generous benefactor and patron of the Arts. Apart from library in Dublin, containing 13,000 volumes left in trust to Irish nation, donated paintings to value of £1 million to National Gallery and unique collection of oriental weapons to Military College, Curragh Camp.

21/1

1876: James Larkin, Labour leader, born in Liverpool, son of impoverished Irish immigrants.

1885: Speech in Cork by Charles Stewart Parnell, Nationalist leader:

We cannot under the British Constitution ask for more than the restitution of Grattan's Parliament, but no man has a right to fix the boundary to the march of a nation. No man has a right to say to his country: 'Thus far shalt thou go and no further'. We have never attempted to fix the *ne plus ultra* to the progress of Ireland's nationhood, and we never shall.

1919: First Dáil Éireann convened in Mansion House, Dublin.

Twenty-seven Sinn Féin MPs in attendance (thirty-four Sinn Féin MPs in prison and eight others absent for other reasons) re-affirmed declaration of independence of 1916, adopted provisional constitution and appointed delegates to attend peace conference of Allied powers in Paris.

: First shots fired in War of Independence.

At Soloheadbeg, Co. Tipperary, a group of Volunteers of third Tipperary Brigade, led by Seán Treacy, Dan Breen and Séamus Robinson, shot dead two members of RIC engaged in escorting cartload of explosives to nearby quarry.

22/1

1632: At Franciscan monastery in Donegal, work began on *Annales Rioghachta Éireann* – the *Annals of the Four Masters* – a chronicle of Irish history from the earliest days to 1616.

Four Masters of popular title, given to *Annals* by Fr John Colgan of Louvain, were all master historians; principally Franciscan lay brother Micheál Ó Cléirigh, assisted by Fearfeasa Ó Maolchonaire, Cúchoigcríche Ó Cléirigh and Cúchoigcríche Ó Duibhgeannain. An invaluable source-book of historical material, *Annals* considered substantially accurate from fifth century onwards.

1913: Cardinal William Conway, Archbishop of Armagh and Primate of All-Ireland (1963–77) born in Belfast.

23/1

1608: Government announced project for plantation of escheated lands in six Ulster counties: Tyrone, Coleraine, Donegal, Fermanagh, Armagh and Cavan.

1803: Death of Arthur Guinness, founder of Guinness' Brewery.

When Dr Arthur Price, Archbishop of Cashel died, in 1752, left £100 each to land steward's two sons, Arthur and Richard Guinness. In 1756, young Arthur leased brewery at Leixlip, Co. Kildare. Later bought brewery at St James' Gate, Dublin, where in 1778, he began to brew porter – dark concoction containing roasted barley and first drunk by London porters. For a time, brew known locally as 'Guinness, black Protestant porter' because of proprietor's opposition to United Irishmen. Subsequently, St James' Gate became largest porter and stout brewery in the world, its 'extra stout porter' becoming known simply as 'stout'.

If clerical money did help launch Arthur Guinness in brewing business, he was generous with profits, as benefactor of religious and charitable institutions. In 1786, founded Ireland's first Sunday school. Of his twenty-one children, ten survived to establish well-known Guinness dynasty.

24/1

1862: Death in Paris of Myles Byrne, United Irishman.

Byrne, born at Monaseed, Co. Wexford, took part in Battles of Arklow and Vinegar Hill. Joined Robert Emmet in aborted rising of 1803. Subsequently sent by Emmet to enlist aid of Napoleon Bonaparte.

Irish Legion formed by Napoleon with view to sending French expedition to Ireland but expedition never materialised. Byrne served with distinction in Napoleonic campaigns of 1804–15 and was made a chevalier of the Legion of Honour.

1971: Death of St John Greer Ervine, dramatist, novelist and poet. Author of many plays including *Mixed Marriage* (1910) and *The First Mrs Frazer* (1928). Novels include *Mrs Martin's Men* and *Changing Winds*.

1973: Death of Willie Clancy, folklorist, master carpenter and renowned musician, particularly on the uilleann pipes.

25/1

1627: Robert Boyle, natural philosopher, born at Lismore Castle, Co. Waterford. Famous for 'Boyle's Law' (1662), that the pressure and the volume of gas are inversely proportional.

1886: Irish Unionist Party formed in House of Commons under leadership of Colonel Edward J. Saunderson to support Conservatives in opposition to first Home Rule Bill.

1917: *Laurentic* disaster.
White Star liner, *Laurentic*, bound for Canada sank off Lough Swilly after being struck twice by U-boat torpedoes. Three hundred and fifty-four perished.

1920: Death of William Percy French, painter and song-writer. Many popular songs include 'The Mountains of Mourne'.

1928: Death of Rev. James Brown Armour, Presbyterian minister, ecumenist and Home Rule supporter, known as 'Armour of Ballymoney'.

26/1

1904: Seán MacBride, revolutionary, politician, Nobel and Lenin

Peace Prize winner, born in Paris.

1907: First production of John Millington Synge's *The Playboy of the Western World* at the Abbey Theatre.

Greeted with serious disorder throughout week-long run. Objections ostensibly centred on use of word 'shift' to describe a woman's nightdress, and Playboy's remark about 'bloody fools'. Considered most objectionable was showing of Ireland in bad light before the world through play's description of young man becoming a hero because he has slain his father.

Newspapers' reaction equally bitter. In *United Irishman* Arthur Griffith asserted that whole affair financed by English money to defame the Irish. *Freeman's Journal* attacked 'this unmitigated protracted libel upon Irish peasant men and worse still, upon Irish peasant girlhood'.

27/1

1834: Death of Roger O'Connor, United Irishman.

Born in Connorville, Co. Cork; imprisoned in 1798 for membership of United Irishmen. On release, rented Dungan Castle, Co Meath – destroyed by fire after he had insured it for £5,000. In 1817, tried and acquitted of robbery of Galway Mail Coach. Later proven to have wasted brother's property, which he held in trust, to the tune of £10,000.

In 1822, published *The Chronicles of Eri*, a 'history of the Irish' translated from 'the original manuscripts of the Phoenician dialect' complete with a portrait of the author with the words 'O'Connor, chief of the prostrated people of this nation'. *The Chronicles of Eri* was mostly his own fiction.

Father of Chartist leader, Feargus O'Connor (1794–1855).

1975: Death of Mother Mary Martin, founder of Medical Missionaries of Mary (1937).

28/1

1807: Robert McClure, explorer who discovered Northwest Passage, born in Wexford.

1829: William Burke, 'body snatcher' was hanged in Edinburgh.

Edinburgh body-snatching case, one of most gruesome in British criminal history, involved two Irishmen, William Burke from Orrery, Co. Cork and William Hare from Derry.

The two migrant labourers conducted a lucrative business by luring obscure wayfarers into their lodging house at Tanner's Close, Edinburgh. Assisted by their wives, disposed of at least fifteen people, usually by making them drunk and then suffocating them, earning from local school of anatomy sums ranging from £8 to £14 for the bodies. Scheme came to light when one of their lodgers found a body in the cellar.

Burke subsequently convicted of murder and hanged. Hare, who turned King's Evidence, left Edinburgh and died years later, an old blind beggar, in London

1939: Death at Roquebrune in the South of France of William Butler Yeats, Ireland's greatest poet. Works include *The Countess Cathleen* (1892), *The Celtic Twilight* (1893), *Poems: Second Series* (1910) and *Later Poems* (1922).

29/1

1852: Louis Brennan, inventor of 'Brennan' dirigible torpedo for coastal defence, born in Castlebar, Co. Mayo.

Brought up in Melbourne, Australia, Brennan sold exclusive rights to invention to British government in 1886, for sum of £100,000. Subsequently worked for British in various defence projects, including work on development of helicopter.

30/1

1845: Katharine ('Kitty') O'Shea, mistress and later wife of Nationalist leader Charles Stewart Parnell, born Katharine Wood at Bradwell, Essex.

1864: National Gallery of Ireland officially opened in Dublin.

1872: Death of Francis Rawden Chesney, soldier and explorer, 'Father of the Suez Canal'.

1947: Death of James Larkin, labour leader and founder of Irish Transport and General Workers' Union (1909).

1972: 'Bloody Sunday' in Derry.

After a banned Civil Rights Association march in city, British troops shot dead thirteen unarmed men, seven aged under 19.

31/1

1913: Ulster Volunteer Force (UVF) formed in Belfast, under command of General Sir George Richardson and Captain Wilfred Spender.

1953: *Princess Victoria* ferry disaster.

The *Princess Victoria*, en route from Stranraer to Larne, Co. Antrim, sank in hurricane-force conditions some 4 miles northeast of New Island at entrance to Belfast Lough. Of hundred and seventy-four passengers and crew on board, only thirty-one survived.

February

1/2

Feast of St Brigid

1815: Duel between Daniel O'Connell and John D'Esterre on estate of Lord Ponsonby at Bishopscourt, Co. Kildare.

When handkerchief fell, D'Esterre declared shot but, perhaps for first time in his life, missed. O'Connell fired a second later and D'Esterre fell to ground. Thought at time that only slightly wounded but died three days later.

O'Connell settled pension on D'Esterre's widow, named eldest daughter after St Brigid and for rest of life wore black glove on his right hand when receiving Eucharist.

1878: Thomas MacDonagh, poet and revolutionary, born at Cloughjordan, Co. Tipperary.

1963: Death of Cardinal John Francis D'Alton, Archbishop of Armagh and Primate of All-Ireland from 1946.

1967: Northern Ireland Civil Rights Association (NICRA) founded in Belfast.

1982: Ban on corporal punishment in Republic of Ireland schools, introduced by Minister of Education, John Boland, came into effect.

2/2

1882: James Joyce, poet, novelist and playwright born in Dublin. Works include *The Portrait of an Artist as a Young Man* (1916).

1922: Death in New York of John Butler Yeats, painter and father of poet William Butler Yeats and artist, Jack Butler Yeats.

3/2

1537: Lord Thomas FitzGerald, tenth Earl of Kildare, better known as 'Silken Thomas' was hanged, drawn and quartered at Tyburn, along with his five uncles.

1862: Thomas Francis Meagher became brigadier-general of Irish Brigade in American Civil War.

Brigade saw action at second battle of Bull Run (August 1862), battle of Antietam Creek (September 1862) and Fredericksburg (December 1862) before annihilation at Chancellorsville (May 1863).

1896: Death of Lady Jane Wilde, writer, often under pen-name 'Speranza'. Succession of works on Irish folklore include *Driftwood from Scandinavia* (1884). Mother of Oscar Wilde.

4/2

1868: Countess Markievicz, revolutionary, born Constance Gore-Booth, in London.

Dominant figure in Cumann na mBan – founded 1911 as auxiliary to Irish Volunteers; served as second-in-command to Michael Mallin in Stephen's Green in Easter 1916. 1918, first woman to be elected to British House of Commons. In first Dáil Éireann, January 1919, first woman in western Europe to be appointed cabinet minister and first ever female minister of labour.

1963: Death of Brinsley MacNamara, real name John Weldon, writer. Notable works include *The Valley of the Squinting Windows* (1918).

1992: President Mary Robinson became first Irish President to visit Belfast.

: In Belfast, off-duty RUC officer killed three occupants of Sinn Féin office, before taking own life.

5/2

1820: Death of William Drennan, poet and United Irishman.

Drennan held to the last to his dream of fusion of Catholic, Protestant and Dissenter. Directed in will that coffin be carried to grave by six Protestants and six Catholics.

1880: Irish Rugby Football Union (IRFU) founded in Dublin.

1921: Death at Littlehampton, Sussex of Katharine O'Shea, mistress and later wife of Nationalist leader, Charles Stewart Parnell.

> The Bishops and the Party
> That tragic story made,
> A husband that had sold his wife
> And after that betrayed;
> But stories that live longest
> Are sung above the glass,
> And Parnell loved his country,
> And Parnell loved his lass.
>
> W.B. Yeats

Katharine O'Shea, described by contemporaries as a woman of average appearance but vivacious personality, survived Parnell by 19 years. No evidence that she ever set foot in Ireland.

1992: Five Catholics killed by Loyalist gunmen in attack on bookmaker's shop in Belfast.

6/2

1968: Death of William Conor, genre and narrative painter, renowned for numerous studies of his native Belfast.

1971: In Belfast, gunner Robert Curtis, aged 20, of Royal Artillery Regiment, became first serving British soldier to be killed since deployment of British army in Northern Ireland in August 1969.

7/2

1642: Death of Bishop William Bedell, co-author of *Bedell's Bible*.

1867: Death of William Dargan, pioneer of Irish railways.

Organised construction of over 600 miles of railway, including first line between Dublin and Kingstown (1831). Also built Ulster Canal, linking Lough Erne and Belfast.

1875: Sir Alfred Chester Beatty, mining engineer, philanthropist, art collector and first honorary citizen of Ireland, born in New York.

1877: Death of John O'Mahony, Gaelic scholar and co-founder of Fenian Brotherhood (1858).

1991: In London, Provisional IRA mortar bomb exploded in garden of No. 10 Downing Street.

8/2

1929: Death of James Connell, writer of socialist anthem 'The Red Flag' and a number of political works.

Connell, born at Killskyre, Co. Meath, wrote 'The Red Flag' during Dock Strike 1889. Subsequently set to old German air 'Tannenbaum'. In 1924, Labour Prime Minister, Ramsay MacDonald held competition to find substitute. However, judges, John McCormack and Sir Hugh Robertson, declared that none of 300 entries could match 'The Red Flag'.

1970: Death of Cahir Healy, Nationalist politician.

Born at Mountcharles, Co. Donegal, held seat for South Fermanagh at Stormont for 40 years. Prolific contributor to print media.

9/2

1854: Edward Carson, lawyer and politician who led opposition to Home Rule for Ireland, born in Dublin.

1903: Death of Sir Charles Gavan Duffy, Young Irelander who later became Prime Minister of Victoria.

1923: Brendan Behan, writer and wit, born in Dublin. Famous for autobiography, *Borstal Boy* (1958) and for plays *The Quare Fellow* (1954) and *The Hostage* (1959).

1926: Garret FitzGerald, Fine Gael leader (1977–87) and twice Taoiseach, born in Dublin, son of Desmond FitzGerald, then Minister for External Affairs.

10/2

1889: Death in Melbourne, Australia of Peter Lalor, colonial politician.

Born in Tinnakill, Co. Laois 1823, younger brother of Young Irelander, James Fintan Lalor. Civil engineer, emigrated to Australia in 1852 shortly after discovery of gold. Took up rich claims in Ballarat, some 150 miles west of Melbourne. Led miners' rebellion at Eureka Stockade, December 1854.

Lost arm in pitched battle with soldiers and police in which thirty miners killed. Left unconscious but later rescued by friends and hidden from police.

When dispute subsided, continued mining interests. When gold field granted parliamentary representation, elected member for Ballarat. Eventually became Speaker of the House.

11/2

1926: At Abbey Theatre, rioting broke out during performance of Seán O'Casey's *The Plough and the Stars.*

The Plough and the Stars could be broadly described as antiwar play, focusing on heroism of Dublin's tenement poor. But, in storm of protest led by widows of Rising, O'Casey accused of desecrating heroes of Easter Week and offending Dublin morality with obscene language and degenerate characters from slums.

Full-scale riot at fourth performance. At point when prostitute Rosie Redmond comes into pub after political meeting, uproar and cries of 'Get her off the stage!' 'It's a disgrace in a Catholic country!' 'There are no women like that in Dublin!' With missiles flying and curtain hurriedly drawn, W.B. Yeats appeared on stage to restore order with famous 'You have disgraced yourselves again' speech, referring to similar disturbances in 1910 at J.M. Synge's *The Playboy of the Western World.*

The Plough continued its run but with police in the house each night.

1992: Albert Reynolds elected Taoiseach by Dáil Éireann, having succeeded Charles J. Haughey as leader of Fianna Fáil.

12/2

1713: Death of Florence MacMoyer, last hereditary keeper of ninth-century *Book of Armagh*.

In 1680, MacMoyer, a schoolmaster, pawned *Book of Armagh* for sum of £5 to pay his way to London. There, in return for promise of estate 'as good as ever your grandfather had', was employed to act as Crown witness at trial of Oliver Plunkett.

Treachery, however, went unrewarded and he was never in a position to redeem the sacred book which eventually found its way to Trinity College.

Florence MacMoyer died in poverty. On account of connection with Archbishop Plunkett's death, was traditionally believed that once a year he was solemnly cursed by the Pope.

1923: Major James Chichester-Clark, Lord Moyola, politician and Prime Minister of Northern Ireland (1969–71), born at Castledawson, Co. Derry.

13/2

1820: Death of Leonard McNally, barrister, playwright, composer, United Irishman and government informer.

McNally one of first members of Society of United Irishmen. In state trials of 1798 and 1803, defence barrister for many of leaders, including Wolfe Tone, Napper Tandy and Robert Emmet. Wrote a number of comedies and comic operas and composed well-known song 'Sweet Lass of Richmond Hill' in praise of first wife, from Richmond in Yorkshire. Role as informer only came to light after his death.

1864: Stephen Gwynn, author and Nationalist, born in Rathfarnham, Co. Dublin. Novels include *The Old Knowledge* (1901) and *The Glade in the Forest* (1907).

1893: Prime Minister W.E. Gladstone introduced Second Home Rule Bill in House of Commons.

Defeated in House of Lords, in September: 419 votes to 41.

1964: Death of Patrick J. Ryan, Co. Limerick-born hammer-throwing champion and Olympic gold medalist for United States (Antwerp, 1920).

14/2

1629: Valentine Greatrakes, also Greatorex, faith-healer, born at
Affane, Co. Waterford.
      Soldiered under Oliver Cromwell in Irish campaign. Initially
touched for scrofula or 'the King's evil'; later extended healing
powers to ague, rheumatism and other diseases. His procedure
was merely to stroke patients with hands, uttering words 'God
Almighty heal thee for His mercy's sake'. Refused payment,
telling patients to give God the praise if they were cured. In
1666, having been ridiculed by medical profession, published
defence of his cures along with over 50 testimonials from
notable contemporaries.

1853: The *Queen Victoria* sank in snowstorm off Howth Head with
loss of fifty-five lives.

1878: Daniel Corkery, teacher and writer, born in Cork city. Writings include *The Hidden Ireland* (1924).

1981: Stardust ballroom disaster.
      Forty-eight died and over a hundred and twenty injured,
many seriously, when fire raged through Stardust ballroom in
Artane, Dublin, during St Valentine's Day dance. Average age
of victims was 18 years.

15/2

1782: Volunteer Convention at parish church, Dungannon, Co.
Tyrone.
      Presided over by Henry Grattan, Henry Flood and Lord
Charlemont. Convention passed resolution that 'the claim of
any other than the King, Lords and Commons of Ireland to
make laws to bind this kingdom is unconstitutional, illegal, and
a grievance'. Grattan got accepted his motion that 'as Irishmen,
Christians and Protestants, we rejoice at the relaxation of the
penal laws against our Roman Catholic fellow-subjects'.

1874 Sir Ernest Shackleton, Antarctic explorer, born at Kilkea, Co.
Kildare.

1971: Decimal Day.
      Irish currency officially changed over to decimal system.

16/2

1759: Death of Bartholomew Mosse, surgeon and philanthropist.

Mosse, born in Maryborough (Portlaoise), pioneered building of two famous hospitals in Dublin. In March 1745, opened hospital to assist deserving poor women in childbirth – first 'lying-in' hospital in world – located in George's Lane; in 1757, opened Rotunda hospital.

1852: Death of William Thompson, naturalist. Major work: *The Natural History of Ireland* (4 vols, 1849-56).

17/2

1978: In Northern Ireland, twelve people died when Provisional IRA incendiary bomb exploded at La Mon Hotel, Comber, Co. Down.

1980: Derrynaflan hoard discovered on site of ruined monastery near Killenaule, Co. Tipperary.

Hoard consisted of some of Ireland's most precious antiquities, including silver chalice, silver paten with stand, gilt bronze ladle and strainer and bronze basin. Find made by Mr Michael Webb and his son, Michael, using metal detectors.

18/2

1366: Statutes of Kilkenny, prescribing laws of demarcation between inhabitants of Pale – Norman-Irish – and those of rest of Ireland, passed by Irish Parliament.

Norman-Irish, among other prohibitions, forbidden to speak Irish, to inter-marry with natives, to entertain Gaelic minstrels, poets and storytellers, to follow Brehon laws, fosterage, and other Gaelic customs.

In the event, Norman-Irish paid little heed to legislation and native Irish still less.

1948: Assembly of Dáil Éireann, in which John A. Costello (Fine Gael) elected Taoiseach in inter-party government.

19/2

1624: Death of Sir Arthur Chichester, chief instigator of Plantation of Ulster, begun in 1608.

1875: In sport, Ireland played their first rugby international.
At Kennington Oval, London, England defeated Ireland by 2 goals and a try to nil, before a crowd of three thousand.

1890: Death of Joseph Biggar, MP for Co. Cavan, who initiated obstructionist campaign waged by Irish members in House of Commons during late 1870s.

1904: Muiris Ó Súilleabháin, writer, born on Great Blasket island, off Co. Kerry coast. Author of *Fiche Blian ag Fás/Twenty Years A-Growing* (1933).

1941: Death of Sir Hamilton Harty, composer and conductor.

20/2

1808: Death of Gerard Lake, English general.
Lake played prominent part in suppression of Insurrection of 1798. Of executions carried out in Wexford in wake of victory at Vinegar Hill, wrote to Lord Castlereagh: 'I really feel severely the being obliged to order so many men out of the world; but I am convinced. If severe and many examples are not made, the rebellion cannot be put a stop to.'

1883: Pádraic Ó Conaire, writer in the Irish language, born in Galway. Chief works include *Deoraidheacht* (1910), *An Chéad Chloch* (1914), *An Crann Géagach* (1919) and *M'Asal Beag Dubh* (1944).

21/2

1803: Edward Despard, conspirator, hanged in London.
Despard, from Co. Laois, executed with six others for conspiracy to overthrow British government. Plan was to set up republican governments in England, Scotland and Ireland.

1823: Death of Rev. Charles Wolfe, poet.
Remembered today for one poem, 'The Burial of Sir John Moore at Corunna', ode inspired by lonely midnight burial of English commander who was mortally wounded at Corunna in January 1809 during Peninsular War:

> Not a drum was heard, not a funeral note,
> As his corse to the rampart we hurried,
> Not a soldier discharged his farewell shot,
> O'er the grave where our hero we buried....

1922: Free State government began recruitment into Civic Guard, later renamed An Garda Síochána.

First commissioner of new unarmed police force was Michael Staines from Co. Mayo. First member was Patrick Joseph Kerrigan, also from Co. Mayo.

22/2

1893: Peadar O'Donnell, novelist, editor and social reformer, born at Meenmore, Co. Donegal. Most famous books include *Islanders* (1928), *There will be Another Day* (1963) and *Proud Island* (1975).

1900: Seán O'Faolain, novelist, short-story writer, critic and biographer, born John Whelan in Cork.

Extensive literary output includes *Midsummer Night Madness* (1932), *Bird Alone* (1936), *The Great O'Neill* (1942), *The Short Story* (1948) and *The Vanishing Hero* (1956).

23/2

1943: Thirty-five orphan girls died in fire at St Joseph's Orphanage, Cavan town.

Fire broke out during night when girls asleep in dormitories Those on second floor trapped as fire engulfed main staircase. Many were injured in jumping to safety. Several girls and one elderly member of staff lost lives trying to save others.

1975: Death of Ernest Blythe, politician and managing director of Abbey Theatre (1941-67).

Blythe, born at Magheragall, near Lisburn, Co. Antrim, became Minister of Finance in 1923, only Northern Protestant to become cabinet minister in Republic. Life-long devotee of Irish language.

24/2

1797: Samuel Lover, poet, novelist and artist, born in Dublin. Most famous novel: *Handy Andy* (1842).

1826: Death of Peter O'Connell, lexicographer.

In researching Irish-English dictionary, travelled extensively in search of rare words and variations, visiting among other places, Scottish Highlands and Hebrides. Acknowledged as greatest Gaelic scholar of his age. Was born and died at Carne, Co. Clare.

Shortly after his death, nephew, Anthony O'Connell took manuscript of dictionary to Daniel O'Connell at Tralee, hoping to draw public attention to it. But Liberator showed no interest and on being told that dictionary took 40 years to complete, dismissed visitor, telling him that his uncle was an old fool to have spent so much of his life on so useless a book. Anthony O'Connell then pawned manuscript for ten shillings to Tralee publican. Subsequently rescued by scholar Eugene O'Curry and eventually sold to British Museum.

1852: George Moore, novelist, closely associated with Irish literary revival and founding of Abbey Theatre, born at Moore Hall, Ballyglass, Co. Galway. Novels include *Esther Waters* (1894).

25/2

1852: Death of Thomas Moore, poet, best remembered for his *Irish Melodies* (1807–34) and as man who destroyed Lord Byron's memoirs.

1967: Death of Samuel John Waddell, playwright and actor under name 'Rutherford Mayne'. Plays include *The Drone* (1908).

26/2

1839: John Pentland Mahaffy, scholar and Provost of Trinity College, Dublin, born in Switzerland of Irish parents.

1914: The *Britannic*, sister ship of the *Olympic* (launched 1910) and the *Titanic* (launched 1911) and largest ship built in these islands, launched at Harland and Wolff's Shipyard in Belfast.

27/2

1792: Irish House of Commons partially destroyed by fire.

Fire, caused by central heating system in building, broke out as MPs discussing how they could encourage populace to drink beer instead of whiskey. Nobody hurt.

1935: Death of Shan Bullock, novelist who wrote about life in his native Co. Fermanagh. Novels include *The Loughsiders* (1924).

1937: Death in Battle of Jarama during Spanish Civil War of 22-year-old Charles Donnelly, poet and revolutionary.

Eighteen other Irish anti-Fascists fell with Donnelly during a month-long battle in which twenty-five thousand members of Republican forces perished.

28/2

1884: Seán MacDiarmada, Republican, born at Kiltyclogher, Co. Leitrim.

1977: Brian Faukner, Unionist leader and last Prime Minister of Northern Ireland prior to imposition of direct rule from Westminster in March 1972, killed in riding accident in Co. Down.

1985: In Northern Ireland, nine members of RUC – seven policemen and two policewomen – killed in Provisional IRA mortar attack on Newry, Co. Down RUC station.

29/2

1743: James Gandon, architect of some of Dublin's finest buildings, including the Four Courts, born in London.

1841: John Philip Holland, inventor who pioneered modern submarine, born in Liscannor, Co. Clare.

March

1889: Richard Pigott, journalist and forger of Parnell letters, shot himself dead while being arrested by British police in hotel room No. 13 at Hotel Embajadores, Madrid.

1965: Remains of Sir Roger Casement, hanged in Pentonville prison in 1916, re-interred in Glasnevin Cemetery, Dublin, after State funeral.

1981: In Northern Ireland, Republican prisoners in Long Kesh prison began phased hunger-strike in support of demands for improved conditions.

Hunger-strike claimed lives of ten prisoners: Bobby Sands, Francis Hughes, Raymond McCreesh, Patsy O'Hara, Joe McDonnell, Martin Hurson, Kevin Lynch, Kieran Doherty, Thomas McIlwee and Micky Devine.

Called off after 217 days on 3 October, after which, Secretary of State for Northern Ireland, James Prior, announced that prisoners would be entitled to wear own clothes and protesters would have half of lost remission restored.

1979: Christy Ring, legendary Cork hurler, died.

Ring played for Cork senior hurling team for first time in 1939 and was still on Munster side which won Railway Cup in 1963. Medal tally included 18 Railway Cup medals, 8 All-Ireland senior hurling and an All-Ireland minor medal in 1938.

3/3

1854: Death of Harriet Constance Smithson Berlioz, actress.

Miss Smithson, who captivated French composer Hector Berlioz when she played rôles of Desdemona and Juliet on Paris stage in 1828, was inspiration behind his *Symphonie fantastique* (1830). Couple married in 1833 but separated by mutual consent in 1840.

1984: Death of 'Rinty' Monaghan, Belfast-born world flyweight boxing champion who retired undefeated.

4/3

1778: Robert Emmet, patriot, born in Dublin, youngest son of Dr Robert Emmet, physician to Viceroy.

1794: William Carleton, novelist, born at Prillisk, near Clogher, Co. Tyrone. Most notable work: *Traits and Stories of the Irish Peasantry* (5 vols, 1830–33).

The history of a nation is not in parliaments and battlefields, but in what the people say to each other on fair days and high days and in how they farm and quarrel and go on pilgrimage. These things has Carleton recorded.

W.B. Yeats

1864: Daniel Mannix, Archbishop of Melbourne (1917–63), born in Charleville, Co. Cork.

1978: Death of General Emmet Dalton, senior officer accompanying Michael Collins when latter shot dead at Béal Na Bláth in August 1922.

5/3

1867: Fenian Rising.

Rising a total failure, though outbreaks occurred in Counties Dublin, Wicklow, Tipperary, Limerick, Clare, Louth and Cork. In Co. Cork, rebels under Captain John McClure captured coastguard station and quantity of arms at Knockadoon.

1921: War of Independence: Clonbanin (Co. Cork) ambush.

Convoy of 5 British military vehicles, including armoured

car, ambushed by men of North Cork and East Kerry IRA, under command of Seán Moylan. In 2-hour gun battle, thirteen British soldiers, including brigadier general, killed and further fifteen wounded. IRA suffered no casualties and a Republican prisoner, being carried by convoy as hostage, succeeded in slipping away to safety.

6/3

1791: John MacHale, Archbishop of Tuam (1834–81) and staunch Nationalist, born at Tobbernavine, Co. Mayo.

1831: Philip Henry Sheridan, United States general, born at Killinkere, Co. Cavan.

1918: Death of John Redmond, Nationalist leader.

1978: Death of Micheál MacLíammóir (born Willmore), actor, playwright and co-founder of Gate Theatre in Dublin.

1988: Gibraltar shootings.
Three unarmed members of Provisional IRA: Máiréad Farrell, Seán Savage and Daniel McCann shot dead by members of SAS in Gibraltar. In September 1988, inquest in Gibraltar returned verdict of 'lawful killing' for all three deaths.

7/3

1923: Ballyseedy Massacre, Co. Kerry
In one of worst atrocities of Irish Civil War, eight Republican prisoners killed when, while they were tied to a log, Free State soldiers threw mine amongst them.

1937: Death of Tomás Ó Criomhthain, Blasket Islander and writer, most famous for *An t-Oileánach/The Islandman* (1929).

8/3

1702: Death, in a fall from his horse, of King William III, formerly Prince of Orange.

1770: Mary Anne McCracken, younger sister of United Irishman Henry Joy McCracken and lover of Thomas Russell, 'The man from God knows where', born in Belfast.

1966: Nelson's Pillar, Dublin's most familiar landmark, demolished in explosion.
    The 120–foot Doric column, surmounted by a 13–foot statue
of Admiral Nelson sculpted by Thomas Kirk RHA and completed in 1808. Explosion – in year which marked fiftieth anni-
versary of Easter Rising – attributed to Republican extremists.

9/3

1771: Thomas Reynolds, informer, born in Dublin.
    Reynolds related through marriage to Wolfe Tone – he and
Tone married to Witherington sisters. Joined United Irishmen
but turned informer when he heard of revolutionary intentions.
Through his information, government able to arrest Leinster
Committee at home of Oliver Bond in March 1798, and so vir-
tually destroy conspiracy.

1932: Seventh Dáil Éireann assembled.
    Eamon De Valera formed first Fianna Fáil government.
Fianna Fáil, under his leadership, remained in office for following sixteen years.

1957: Sixteenth Dáil Éireann assembled.
    Fianna Fáil returned to office with Eamon De Valera as Taoi-
seach.

1982: Twenty-third Dáil Éireann assembled.
    Fianna Fail took office with Charles J. Haughey as Taoi-
seach.

10/3

1653: Sir Phelim O'Neill, commander of Irish forces in Ulster during rebellion of 1641, was executed in Dublin.

1888: Barry Fitzgerald, acclaimed character actor, born William
Joseph Shields in Dublin.

1894: In rugby, Ireland won her first Triple Crown, defeating
Wales by penalty goal to nil, in Belfast.

1966: Death of Frank O'Connor (pseudonym of Michael O'Donovan), writer, best known for his short stories, including collection *Guests of the Nation* (1931).

1987: Twenty-fifth Dáil Éireann assembled.
Fianna Fáil returned to office under Charles J. Haughey as Taoiseach.

11/3

1596: One hundred and twenty-six people killed when cargo of gunpowder barrels exploded at Wood Quay, Dublin.

1857: Thomas James Clarke, senior of 1916 Proclamation signatories, born of Irish parents at Hurst Castle, Isle of Wight.

12/3

1685: George Berkeley, metaphysical philosopher and educationalist, born at Dysart Castle, Thomastown, Co. Kilkenny.

1689: King James II landed at Kinsale, Co. Cork accompanied by French fleet and hundred French officers.

13/3

1846: Evictions at Ballinglass, Co. Galway.
In early morning, large detachment of infantry accompanied by sheriff and a number of police descended on Ballinglass, a village of sixty-one houses. Three hundred inhabitants called upon to give up possession and homes systematically demolished. That night, villagers slept in the ruins. Following day, driven out, foundations of houses torn up and razed and no neighbour permitted to take them in. Tenants of Ballinglass not in arrears with rent and had, by own efforts, successfully reclaimed some 400 acres from neighbouring bog. Misfortune lay in coming between landowner, Mrs Gerard, and her plan to turn holdings into a grazing farm.
Despite widespread condemnation and debate in House of Lords, evictions not rescinded.

14/3

1738: John Beresford, statesman, once described as 'virtual King of Ireland', born in Dublin.

1921: War of Independence: six Republicans executed in Mountjoy jail.

Thomas Bryan, Patrick Doyle, Frank Flood and Bernard
Ryan convicted of 'high treason by levying war'. Thomas
Whelan and Patrick Moran convicted of participation in execu-
tion of British agents on Bloody Sunday, November 1920.

1973: Twentieth Dáil Éireann assembled.

Liam Cosgrave elected Taoiseach at head of Fine Gael–
Labour coalition government.

15/3

1852: Lady Gregory, playwright, folklorist and co-founder of
Abbey Theatre, born Isabella Augusta Persse at Roxbor-
ough, Co. Galway. Published works include *Cuchulain of
Muirthemne* (1902) and *The Rising of the Moon* (1903).

1895: Manslaughter of Brigid Cleary – 'Tipperary Witchcraft
Case'.

Brigid Cleary killed in own home, near village of Fethard,
Co. Tipperary by husband, Michael. Believed she was not his
real wife but another woman, a 'changeling', substituted in her
place by fairies. She died from shock when her husband, in fit
of rage at her refusal to take three slices of bread before tasting
her tea – a popular charm – poured lamp oil over her clothes
and set them alight. Scene witnessed by a number of family
friends and relations. Ten charged at Clonmel Court with her
murder. Most given short terms of imprisonment. Michael
Cleary sentenced to 20 years penal servitude, charge against
him having been reduced from murder to manslaughter.

16/3

1789: Francis Rawdon Chesney, soldier and explorer renowned as
'Father of the Suez Canal' born at Annalong, Co. Down.

1839: John Butler Yeats, subject and portrait painter and father of
poet W.B. Yeats and artist Jack B. Yeats, born at Tullylish,
Co. Down.

1907: Death of John O'Leary, Fenian.

> Romantic Ireland's dead and gone,
> It's with O'Leary in the grave.

> from 'September 1916'
> by W.B. Yeats

1960: P and O liner, *Canberra*, launched at Belfast shipyards.
The *Canberra* (45,000 tons) was last large liner built in Belfast. Launch marked end of post-war ship-building boom.

17/3
St Patrick's Day

1777: Patrick Brontë, clergyman and father of literary Brontë sisters born at Ballinaskeagh, near Loughbrickland, Co. Down.

1778: Volunteer companies started in Belfast, with Lord Charlemont as commander of Northern Volunteers.

1779: First St Patrick's Day parade in New York.

1841: Death, aboard steamer, *President*, when she foundered off Cape Cod, of Tyrone Power, actor and playwright; grandfather of cinema actor Tyrone Power and theatrical producer Sir Tyrone Guthrie.

1858: Irish Republican Brotherhood (IRB) or Fenian movement launched in Dublin by James Stephens.

1870: Death, aged 24, of John Keegan Casey, Fenian, poet and balladeer. Work includes 'The Rising of the Moon'.

1889: Harry Clarke, illustrator and stained-glass designer, born in Dublin.

18/3
1768: Death of Laurence Sterne, writer. Works include *Tristram Shandy* (1760).

1800: Harriet Constance Smithson, latterly Madame Berlioz, actress, born in Ennis, Co. Clare, daughter of theatre manager.

19/3

1824: William Allingham, poet, born in Ballyshannon, Co. Donegal.

1921: War of Independence: Crossbarry, West Cork, engagement.
IRA flying column under General Tom Barry achieved one of most celebrated rebel successes of war by fighting their way out of encircling military movement and inflicting heavy casualties on Crown forces. General Sir Nevil Macready, Commander of British army in Ireland, described engagement, which lasted about 2 hours, as nearest approaching actual warfare, as contrasted with previous ambushes.

20/3

1875: Death in Newry, Co. Down of John Mitchel, patriot and author of *Jail Journal* (1854).

1914: 'Curragh Mutiny' affair.
Fifty-seven British officers, under leadership of Major General Sir Hubert Gough, stationed at Curragh Camp, Co. Kildare, decided to resign commissions if ordered to move against Ulster Volunteer Force. Such orders were never issued.

1920: Tomás MacCurtain, Lord Mayor of Cork, murdered in his home.
In April 1920 coroner's jury returned verdict of wilful murder against Royal Irish Constabulary.

1964: Death, aged 41, of Brendan Behan, wit and writer. Works include *The Quare Fellow* (1954) and autobiography *Borstal Boy* (1958).

1971: In Northern Ireland, six people died and thirty-one were injured when series of car bombs exploded in Belfast.

21/3

1884: Nora Barnacle, mistress and later wife of writer James Joyce, born in Galway workhouse hospital.

1920: Death of An t-Athair Peadar Ó Laoghaire, writer in Irish. Work includes folk-novel *Séadna* (1904) and autobiography *Mo Scéal Féin* (1915).

1978: Death of Cearbhall Ó Dálaigh, lawyer, academic, and fifth President of Ireland (1974–6).

22/3

1835: Death of Alexander Pope, actor and painter.

Pope, born in Cork, was a leading actor on London stage for over 40 years. Speciality was tragedy and his Othello was unrivalled in his day. Throughout his life, continued to paint, having began his career executing portraits at a guinea a time.

Married in turn three woman of considerable fortune, but rarely free from financial difficulties because of appetite for good living. At time of his death, was living off a pension of £100 a year from a theatre charity.

1848: Sarah Purser, artist, born at Kingstown (Dún Laoghaire), Co. Dublin.

23/3

1868: Prime Minister W.E. Gladstone proposed end to establishment of Church of Ireland.

Prior to subsequent Irish Church Act, 1869, members of Established Church – Church of Ireland – enjoyed civil and political privileges denied to others. Catholics, Presbyterians and other non-conformist Christians, in law, nothing better than second-class citizens. Catholics scarcely citizens at all.

Act also abolished contentious tithe system whereby all compelled by law to pay for upkeep of Church of Ireland and its clergy.

1889: Robert John Gibbings, wood-engraver, book designer and author, born in Cork. Author of *Lovely is the Lee* (1945) and *Sweet Cork of Thee* (1951).

1971: In Northern Ireland, Brian Faulkner became leader of Unionist Party and Prime Minister.

1983: Death of Constantine Fitzgibbon, writer. Works include *The Arabian Bird* (1948), *The Blitz* (1957) and *The Life and Times of Eamon de Valera* (1973).

24/3

1909: Death, at age 38, of John Millington Synge, playwright. Works include *The Shadow of the Glen* (1903), *Riders to the Sea* (1904) and *The Playboy of the Western World* (1907).

1922: In Belfast, the McMahon Murders took place.
    Owen McMahon, a Catholic publican, his six sons and a barman shot dead by Protestant paramilitaries. Murders carried out in revenge for killing of two policemen in city previous day by anti-Treaty IRA faction.

1968: Tuskar Rock air-disaster, Co. Wexford.
    Aer Lingus viscount, the *St Phelim*, on routine flight between Cork and London, crashed into sea near Tuskar Rock with loss of all sixty-one passengers and crew on board. Republic of Ireland's worst aviation disaster. Cause of crash never established.

1972: In Northern Ireland, Stormont administration suspended.
    Following refusal of Prime Minister Brian Faulkner and his cabinet to accept transfer of security powers to Westminster, British government announced that Northern Ireland parliament at Stormont would be prorogued from 30 March.

25/3

1738: Death of Turlough Carolan, harper and last of traditional Irish bards.
    Lamented by ten harpers, Carolan buried at Kilronan, Lough Meelagh, after wake lasting four days.

1831: Arthur MacMorrough Kavanagh, landlord and MP, born at Borris, Co. Carlow.
    Despite being born severely handicapped, with just rudiments of arms and legs, Kavanagh adept at riding, shooting,

fishing, painting and sailing. Philanthropic works included re-building of villages of Borris and Ballyragget and provision of Catholic chapel in New Ross workhouse.

1846: Michael Davitt, founder of Irish National Land League (1879), born at Straide, Co. Mayo, son of a small farmer.

1920: Arrival in Ireland of 'Black and Tans', former British army soldiers recruited as reinforcements to RIC.

1978: In sport, John Treacy of Ireland won world cross-country championship in Glasgow.

1986: Death of Eddie McAteer, leader of Nationalist Party in Northern Ireland (1953–70).

26/3

1856: William Ferguson Massey, Prime Minister of New Zealand (1912–25), born at Limavady, Co. Derry.

1932: Death of Sir Horace Plunkett, pioneer of agricultural co-operation and founder, in 1894, of Irish Agricultural Organisation Society.

27/3

1858: Death of John Hogan, sculptor.
    Born in Tallow, Co. Waterford, studied in Rome, at school of St Luke, and Galleries of Vatican and Capital. Best known works include statue of Fr Theobald Mathew in Cork city and 'Dead Christ' in Clarendon Street Church, Dublin.

28/3

1820: Sir William Howard Russell, first 'modern war correspondent', born in Tallaght, Co. Dublin.
    The 'thin red streak', phrase he used to describe Russian infantry at Battle of Balaclava (1854) has become part of English language as 'the thin red line'.

1833: Death at his birthplace, Rosscarbery, Co. Cork, of William

Thompson, political economist and first writer to regard just distribution of wealth as a cardinal principle in political economy. Works include *An Inquiry into the Principles of the Distribution of Wealth most conducive to Human Happiness* (1824).

1957: Death of Jack B. Yeats, artist, writer and brother of poet W.B. Yeats.

Only twentieth-century Irish painter of indisputably European stature, has become exceedingly popular in recent years. In September 1989, one of his paintings, *The Harvest Moon*, sold by private treaty for record price of £280,000.

29/3

1793: Death of Charlotte Brooke, author.

Thanks to her, many of old songs and poems of Ulster have survived. In 1789 – year of French Revolution – she published *Reliques of Irish Poetry*, collection of odes, elegies and songs translated into English verse along with original Irish versions.

Sole surviving daughter of writer Henry Brooke and close friend of novelist Maria Edgeworth. Ancestor of Lord Brookeborough, Prime Minister of Northern Ireland (1943–63).

1873: Peig Sayers, storyteller and subject of autobiography, *Peig* (1936), born at Vicarstown, Dunquin, Co. Kerry.

30/3

1603: Treaty of Mellifont – Hugh O'Neill, Earl of Tyrone, formally submitted to Lord Mountjoy at Mellifont, Co. Louth.

By terms of treaty, O'Neill renounced title, abjured dependence on any foreign power, especially Spain, and resigned all lands and lordships save such as Crown might grant him. His submission brought Gaelic and feudal Ireland to an end and opened Ulster, last unconquered province, to English law and government.

1880: Sean O'Casey, playwright, born in Dublin. Works include *The Shadow of a Gunman* (1923), *Juno and the Paycock* (1924) and *The Plough and the Stars* (1926).

1922: Craig-Collins Pact agreed in London.

Sir James Craig, Prime Minister of Northern Ireland, agreed to recruit Catholics into Special Constabulary and to reinstate Catholics in jobs in Belfast shipyards. Michael Collins, Chairman of Provisional Government, agreed to act against IRA units operating against North from South. Neither side delivered on undertakings.

1979: Assassination of Airey Neave MP.

Neave, Conservative Party spokesman on Northern Ireland, killed by INLA car-bomb in House of Commons underground car park.

31/3

1871: Arthur Griffith, political leader, born in Dublin.

Founder of Sinn Féin (1905) and leader of Irish plenipotentiaries to negotiations which resulted in Anglo–Irish Treaty of December 1921. Views on Irish nationalism were free from racist undertones in so much as he defined an Irishman as one who regarded Ireland as his country and was prepared to work for it.

1914: Death of Timothy D. Sullivan, politician and poet.

Born in Bantry, Co. Cork, is perhaps best remembered for two songs: 'God Save Ireland' (1867) in commemoration of Manchester Martyrs, and 'The Song of the Canadian Backwoods' or 'Ireland, Boys, Hooray', sung by both northern and southern troops on eve of battle of Fredericksburg (December 1862) in American Civil War.

April

1/4

1888: At Birr, Co. Offaly, first All-Ireland hurling final contested. Tipperary, represented by Thurles, defeated Galway, represented by Meelick, with score of 1–1 to 0–0. Twenty-one players on each team.

1966: Death of Brian O'Nolan, alias 'Flann O'Brien' and 'Myles na gCopaleen', author, newspaper columnist and master of comic invention. Works include *At-Swim-Two-Birds* (1939), *The Third Policeman* (1967) and *An Béal Bocht* (published posthumously, 1973).

2/4

1902: Death of Ethna Carbery, pen-name of Anna MacManus, née Johnston, writer who did much to stimulate Sinn Féin movement. Works include *The Four Winds of Eirinn* (1902) and *In the Celtic Past* (1904), as well as the ballad 'Roddy MacCorley'.

1972: Launch of Raidió Na Gaeltachta, subsidiary of Radio Telefís Éireann, to serve Irish-speaking regions of Ireland.

1989: President Mikhail Gorbachov of Soviet Union made 2-hour stopover at Shannon Airport – first ever Soviet leader to visit Ireland.

3/4

1769: Death at Forkhill, Co. Armagh, of Peadar Ó Doirnín, Gaelic poet.

1846: Death of Michael Moran, balladeer known as 'Zozimus'.
     Moran, from Liberties district of Dublin, blinded by small-pox when an infant. Became known as Zozimus because of ability to recite history of St Mary of Egypt and the fifth century holy man, Zozimus.

4/4

1774: Death of Oliver Goldsmith, essayist, dramatist, novelist and poet. Works include *The Good Natured Man* (1768) and *She Stoops to Conquer* (1773).

1818: Thomas Mayne Reid, writer of over 30 adventure novels based on own experiences, born at Ballyroney, Co. Down. Works include *Headless Horseman* (1865) and *The Castaways* (1870).

5/4

1855: Dublin–Belfast railway line completed.

1869: Margaret Tennant, pioneer in public social work in Britain, born in Dublin.
     In 1893, became Britain's first female factory inspector and during First World War was chief adviser on women's welfare in ministry of munitions.

1921: Royal Ulster Constabulary (RUC), established under Government of Ireland Act, became operational.

6/4

1926: Rev. Ian Kyle Paisley, moderator of Free Presbyterian Church, leader of Democratic Unionist Party, Westminster MP and MEP, born in Armagh.

1951: 'Mother and Child' scheme, planned by Minister for Health, Dr Noel Browne, dropped by Fine Gael–Clann Na Poblachta cabinet, 2 days after it was condemned by RC bishops.

Proposal, to provide free health care for mothers and all children up to age 16, replaced by means-tested health care 'in conformity with Catholic social teaching'.

1972: Publication of Scarman Tribunal report, investigating acts of violence and civil disturbances in Northern Ireland between March and August 1969.

Found that there was no plot to overthrow government or to mount armed insurrection. Riots, it concluded, were 'communal disturbances' arising from complex political, social and economic situation.

7/4

1868: Thomas D'Arcy McGee, writer and nationalist, assassinated outside home in Ottawa, Canada.

McGee, who left Ireland after Rising of 1848, was member of legislative assembly of Province of Canada. Regarded as father of Canadian Federation. A Fenian and former British soldier, Patrick Joseph Phelan, subsequently hanged for murder.

In July 1991, memorial to McGee unveiled in native Carlingford, Co. Louth by Canadian Prime Minister, Brian Mulroney.

1941: First German bombing of Northern Ireland; thirteen killed.

1973: Death of John Charles McQuaid, Archbishop of Dublin (1940–72).

8/4

1834: Death of Sir Jonah Barrington, politician and writer. Works include *Personal Sketches of his own Time* (3 vols, 1827–32).

1861: Derryveagh evictions, Co. Donegal.

John George Adair, owner of Glenveagh, Gartan and Derryveagh estates – some 28,000 acres in all – evicted forty-seven families, a total of two hundred and forty-four men, women and children, and destroyed their dwellings.

In January 1862, a hundred and twenty-five of those evicted from Derryveagh, and a hundred and thirty evicted from Lord George Hill estate in Gweedore set sail for Australia, having accepted free passage from Government of Victoria.

1886: Prime Minister W.E. Gladstone introduced First Irish Home Rule Bill.

Bill subsequently defeated on second reading in House of Commons, by 341 votes to 311.

9/4

1917: Vincent O'Brien, horse-trainer, born near Kanturk, Co. Cork.

Won 3 successive Cheltenham Gold Cups, with Cottage Rake (1948–50), trained 3 Grand National winners (Early Mist, Royal Tan, Quare Times) and 6 Epsom Derby winners (Larkspur, Sir Ivor, Nijinsky, Roberto, The Minstrel and Golden Fleece).

1926: Gerry Fitt, latterly Lord Fitt, politician, born in Belfast.

1947: Death of Desmond FitzGerald, revolutionary, politician and father of Garret FitzGerald, Fine Gael leader (1977–87).

1981: In Northern Ireland, Bobby Sands, on hunger strike in Long Kesh prison, won Fermanagh–South Tyrone by-election, defeating Official Unionist candidate, Harry West.

10/4

1838: At public meeting in Cork, Fr Theobald Mathew signed pledge of total abstinence with words 'Here goes in the name of the Lord'.

Temperance campaign met with spectacular, though short-lived success. In space of 3 years persuaded over half population to take pledge. Failed to keep his movement non-political and strictly confined to temperance issue and unable to prevent Daniel O'Connell harnessing it to Repeal movement. Left to Pioneer Association, established 1898–1901, to produce successful and long-running abstinence movement. Today, Ireland has largest proportion of teetotallers outside Islamic countries.

1865: Oliver Sheppard, sculptor, born at Cookstown, Co. Tyrone. Works include 'The Death of Cuchulainn', executed 1911–12 and subsequently selected as memorial to 1916 Rising for GPO, Dublin.

1867: George William Russell, poet, theosophist, agricultural economist, editor and essayist, better known by pseudonym 'Æ', born in Lurgan, Co. Armagh. Works include *The Divine Vision* (1904), *The Renewal of Youth* (1911) and *The Interpreters* (1922).

1923: General Liam Lynch, chief-of-staff of Irregular/Republican forces during Civil War, shot dead by Free State troops in the Knockmealdown Mountains, Co. Tipperary.

11/4

1971: At annual congress, held in Belfast, Gaelic Athletic Association (GAA) voted to lift ban on members playing or attending 'foreign games'.

Highlight in application of controversial 'ban' was expulsion, in 1938, of Dr Douglas Hyde, President of Ireland and Patron of GAA, for attending international soccer match at Dalymount Park, Dublin.

12/4

1816: Sir Charles Gavan Duffy, Young Irelander, co-founder of *The Nation* (1842) and Prime Minister of Victoria (1871), born in Monaghan.

1928: The *Bremen* set out from Baldonnel Airfield on first successful east–west flight across Atlantic.

Three-man crew consisted of Germans, Baron von Heunefeld and Captain Kohl, and Dubliner, Major James Fitzmaurice. They landed on Greenly Island off Labrador, 36.5 hours later.

13/4

1742: First public performance of Handel's *Messiah* – conducted by composer himself – took place at New Music Hall, Fishamble Street, Dublin.

1825: Thomas D'Arcy McGee, writer and nationalist, born in Carlingford, Co. Louth. Works include *Irish Writers of the 17th Century* (1847) and a *Life of Art MacMurrough* (1847).

1829: Emancipation Bill, removing last of penal laws from statute book, received Royal assent.

1906: Samuel Beckett, writer, playwright and 1969 winner of Nobel Prize for Literature, born at Foxrock, Co. Dublin. Works include *Murphy* (1938), *Watt* (1944) and *Waiting for Godot* (1953).

1920: Liam Cosgrave, Fine Gael politician and Taoiseach (1973–7) born in Dublin.

1939: Seamus Heaney, poet, born at Bellaghy, Co. Derry. Collections include *Death of a Naturalist* (1966), *North* (1975) and *Station Island* (1984).

1953: Death of Alice Milligan, poet and cultural revivalist whose writings did much to stimulate early Sinn Féin movement. Works include *Life of Wolfe Tone* (1898) and *The Last Feast of the Fianna* (1900).

14/4

1859: Death of Lady Sydney Owenson Morgan, novelist and activist in cause of Catholic emancipation. Works include *The Wild Irish Girl* (1806) and *Florence Macarthy* (1819).

1873: Death of Henry Blosse Lynch, Mesopotamian explorer.
    Born in Ballinrobe, Co. Mayo, joined Indian navy at age of 16 and was second-in-command to Col. Francis Rawdon Chesney on expedition in 1834 to explore Euphrates route to India. In 1837, took over command and became first man to ascend Tigris to Baghdad. During second Burmese War, commanded squadron of Indian navy and, following Persian War 1856–7, conducted negotiations which resulted in Treaty of Paris.

15/4

1864: First Dublin Horse Show, organised by Royal Agricultural Society, took place.

1908: Denis Devlin, diplomat and one of Ireland's greatest poets, born at Greenock, Scotland. Collections include *Inter-*

cessions (1937) and *Lough Derg* (1964).

1912: White Star luxury liner, *Titanic*, sank off Newfoundland.
On maiden voyage from Southampton to New York, sank at 2.20 a.m. having struck iceberg at 11.40 p.m. Of two thousand two hundred and seven passengers and crew aboard, over fifteen hundred perished including a hundred and eighty-seven Irish, mainly young emigrants who had embarked at Queenstown (Cobh, Co. Cork).

1941: First German bombing of Belfast.
At approximately 10.40 p.m. scores of German aircraft flew in over Belfast Lough, raining incendiaries, bombs and parachute mines, mainly on civilian areas. In less than 5 hours over seven hundred died, higher casualty figure than any in Britain, excepting London, for single air raid during Second World War. Fact that Germans returned within 3 weeks indicates that first raid badly executed rather than designed to kill civilians.

16/4

1660: Sir Hans Bartholomew Sloane, naturalist, private physician to King George I, and founder of collection which formed basis of British Museum, born at Killyleagh, Co. Down.

1752: First regular stage-coach service between Dublin and Belfast came into operation.
Drawn by six horses, coach covered the 100-mile journey in three days.

1871: John Millington Synge, playwright, born at Rathfarnham, Co. Dublin. *The Playboy of the Western World* (1907) considered to be his masterpiece.

17/4

1689: Siege of Derry began: dismissal of Governor Robert Lundy.
Word 'Lundy' – derogatory term for Protestant who weakens in fervour for 'Protestant cause' – originates from this Governor of Derry, who, for what he did, or rather didn't do as Jacobites approached city in spring 1689, has gone down in Ulster loyalist tradition as a traitor.
When news of King James' approach reached city, Lundy

called council of war and, having pointed out small means for defence, recommended immediate surrender as wisest course of action. However, majority of inhabitants, led by Rev. George Walker, determined to hold out, leading to famous siege. Lundy declared a traitor and, under imminent danger, was forced to flee city in disguise of a common soldier.

Nevertheless, fact remains that he did not subsequently join Stuart armies. Instead, turned up in London, was held in Tower for a time but later served Crown as a soldier, until death in 1717.

1969: In Northern Ireland, Bernadette Devlin won mid-Ulster by-election at age 21.

In winning by-election Miss Devlin became youngest MP at Westminster, youngest woman MP ever there and youngest MP elected by universal suffrage.

1977: Death of Cardinal William Conway, Archbishop of Armagh since 1963.

18/4

1785: Royal Irish Academy, premier learned institution of Ireland, founded by James Caulfield, first Earl of Charlemont.

1949: (*Easter Monday*): Republic of Ireland formally inaugurated.

Under terms of Republic of Ireland Act, designed by John A. Costello's coalition government to 'take the gun out of Irish politics', Ireland declared to be a Republic and taken out of British Commonwealth. In response, British government passed Ireland Act (1949), recognising Republic but declaring that Northern Ireland or any portion of it would never be detached from UK without consent of its government.

1952: Death of Edward O'Brien, yachtsman and author.

First Irishman to circumnavigate globe in own yacht. On 20 June 1923 at 4.30 p.m. he sailed from Dún Laoghaire in ketch *Saoirse*, bound for New Zealand where he intended to join mountaineering party. Having arrived too late, sailed on via Cape Horn, returning to Dún Laoghaire at precisely 4.30 p.m. on 20 June 1925.

19/4

1876: Death of Sir William Wilde, surgeon, antiquary and father of Oscar Wilde.

1927: First greyhound track in Ireland opened at Celtic Park, Belfast.

20/4

1784: Death of Honoria (Nano) Nagle, founder of Presentation Order of nuns.

1879: First Land League meeting took place at Irishtown, Co. Mayo.
Organised by Michael Davitt and local Fenians, meeting was attended by a crowd of ten thousand.

1896: First screening of a cinema film in Ireland.
Film, using Lumière process, took place at Dan Lowry's Star of Erin Palace of Varieties in Dublin.

1912: Death of Abraham ('Bram') Stoker, Dublin-born novelist. Best remembered for internationally-renowned *Dracula* (1897).

1954: Michael Manning became last man to be judicially executed in Republic of Ireland.
Manning, a 25-year-old carter from Limerick City, hanged in Mountjoy jail for murder of elderly nurse.

21/4

1874: Walter Wilson, engineer and designer of Hallford lorry, extensively used by British army in First World War, born at Blackrock, Co. Dublin.

1916: Sir Roger Casement arrested by Crown forces only hours after embarking from German submarine at Banna Strand, Co. Kerry.

1970: In Northern Ireland, Alliance Party – representing combination of Unionists, Catholic liberals and New Ulster movement – launched.

22/4

1838: The *Sirius* reached Sandy Hook, New York to become first ship to cross Atlantic using steam power only, having left Queenstown, now Cobh, Co. Cork on 4 April.

Sirius commanded by Richard Roberts, Royal Navy lieutenant from Passage West, Co. Cork and manned by crew nearly half of whom were Irish. Vessel belonged to St George Steam Packet Company, world's second steam navigation company, founded in 1821 by group of Corkmen with associates in Dublin and Liverpool. Arrived in New York 8 hours before her rival, Brunel's *Great Western*.

1905: Death of Captain William O'Shea, politician, adventurer and first husband of Katharine O'Shea.

1967: Death of Walter Macken, actor, dramatist and novelist. Works include *Quench the Moon* (1948), *Rain on the Wind* (1950), and *Seek the Fair Land (1959)*.

23/4

1014: (*Good Friday*): Battle of Clontarf.

Brian Bóru, King of Ireland, with army made up almost entirely of Munstermen, faced Leinster Norse, led by Máel Mórda, supported by kinsmen from Northumbria, Isle of Man, Orkneys and further afield. After day-long fighting, Munstermen prevailed and Norse rule in Ireland forever broken.

Brian, too old for battle, was hacked to death in tent by a fleeing Norseman, Brodir. Body subsequently borne to Armagh Cathedral and buried there near high alter.

1792: Thomas Romney Robinson, mathematical physicist and astronomer in charge of Armagh Observatory (1823–82), born in Dublin.

24/4

1718: Nathaniel Hone (the elder), portrait painter, born in Dublin.

1764: Thomas Addis Emmet, United Irishman and older brother of Robert Emmet, born in Cork.

1896: Frederick Robert Higgins, poet, born at Foxford, Co. Mayo. Collections include *Salt Air* (1924), *Arable Holdings* (1933) and *The Gap of Brightness* (1940).

1914: Ulster Volunteer Force gun-running at Ulster ports of Larne, Bangor and Donaghadee.

In spectacular operation organised by Major Fred Crawford, over 20,000 German rifles and 3,000,000 rounds of ammunition landed from the *Clyde Valley* for use by UVF.

However, because of outbreak of First World War and subsequent 'exclusion of Ulster' in 1920, arms never required to oppose Home Rule. Unhappy with cost of storing and guarding arsenal, Stormont government eventually sold it off to Ministry of Supply in Britain at onset of Second World War.

1916: The Easter Rising began.

Irishmen and Irishwomen, in the name of God and the dead generations from which she receives her old tradition of nationhood, Ireland, through us, summons her children to her flag and strikes for her freedom.

From the 1916 Proclamation

Fatal casualties over 5 days of Rising were fifty-six Irish Volunteers; one hundred and three British army personnel; seventeen police; over two hundred civilian non-combatants.

Some two thousand, five hundred were injured, the vast majority civilians.

25/4

1681: Death of Redmond O'Hanlon, Ulster outlaw.

When family dispossessed of extensive estates in Ulster under Cromwellian Settlement, Redmond O'Hanlon took to the road at head of band of tories and kept counties of Armagh and Tyrone in constant state of terror. Authorities made concerted efforts to apprehend him, but he proved an elusive quarry. In his latter years, was under constant threat of arrest, particularly after murder, in 1679, of Captain Henry St John who resided on confiscated O'Hanlon land at Tandragee, Co. Armagh.

Though regarded as folk-hero, evidence suggests that he

attempted, in 1680, to solicit clemency from authorities in return for betraying comrades. Efforts, however, failed. Died a year later, shot by foster brother, Art, at Eightmilebridge, Co. Down.

1819: Vere Foster, philanthropist and educationalist, born in Copenhagen, where Irish-born father was British minister.

26/4

1916: Francis Sheehy-Skeffington, writer, pacifist and socialist, shot dead in Dublin.

Typical of Sheehy-Skeffington that during Easter Week 1916 he walked around streets of Dublin trying to dissuade people from looting. In so doing, arrested by Captain Bowen-Colthurst whom he witnessed killing unarmed boy for breaking curfew. Following morning, along with two journalists, Thomas Dickson and Patrick McIntyre, was executed on Bowen-Colthurst's orders.

In course of time, a senior officer in same barracks reported incident to Prime Minister. Bowen-Colthurst court-martialled and found guilty of murder but declared to have been of unstable mind at time of crime. Former aide-de-camp to Viceroy of Ireland, he was released after a year in Broadmoor Asylum and went on to become a successful banker in Vancouver. He died in 1965.

27/4

1904: Cecil Day-Lewis, critic, novelist (under pseudonym Nicholas Blake) and English poet laureate (1968) born at Ballinturbert, Co. Laois. Work includes *Whisper in the Gloom* (1954), *Buried Day* (1960) and *Requiem for the Living* (1964).

1938: Seanad Éireann, as re-organised under Constitution of 1937, met for first time.

1953: Death, in Dublin, of Maud Gonne MacBride, revolutionary and inspiration for many of works of William Butler Yeats.

28/4

1943: In Northern Ireland, John Andrews resigned as Prime

Minister and leader of Unionist Party.

Andrews, Prime Minister since 1940, succeeded by Sir Basil Brooke.

1969: In Northern Ireland, Captain Terence O'Neill announced resignation as Prime Minister and leader of the Unionist Party.

Captain O'Neill, Prime Minister since 1963, succeeded by Major James Chichester-Clark.

29/4

1680: First stone laid by Duke of Ormond, for Royal Hospital, Kilmainham, Dublin, for soldiers of Irish army.

1769: Arthur Wellesley, first Duke of Wellington and Field Marshal, born in Dublin.

1803: Cardinal Paul Cullen, Archbishop of Dublin and vehement anti-Fenian, born at Prospect, Co. Kildare.

1888: At Clonskeagh, Dublin, first All-Ireland football final contested.

Limerick (Commercials) defeated Dundalk (Young Irelands) with score of 1–4 to 0–3.

1901: Death of James Stephens, founder of Fenian Movement (1858).

30/4

1919: Death of John Pentland Mahaffy, scholar and Provost of Trinity College, Dublin.

1970: In Northern Ireland, Ulster Defence Regiment (UDR) took over duties of abolished Ulster Special Constabulary ('B' Specials).

In July 1992, UDR merged with Royal Irish Rangers to form Royal Irish Regiment.

May

1/5

1170: Norman Invasion of Ireland began.
Small force, under command of Robert FitzStephen, landed at Baginbun, Co. Wexford. Their mission: to help Diarmaid Mac Murchada retrieve kingship of Leinster.

1171: Death at Ferns, Co. Wexford of above Diarmaid Mac Murchada, King of Leinster and the Foreigners.

1316: Edward Bruce, brother of King Robert Bruce of Scotland, crowned King of Ireland at Knockmelan, near Dundalk, Co. Louth.

1780: Amhlaoibh Ó Súilleabháin (Humphrey O'Sullivan), diarist, born in Killarney, Co. Kerry, son of a hedgeschool master.

1803: James Clarence Mangan, poet, born in Dublin. Most famous poem is 'Dark Rosaleen'.

1854: Percy French, painter and songwriter, born at Cloonyquin, Co. Roscommon.

2/5

1858: Edith Œnone Somerville, literary partner of Violet Martin (Martin Ross), born in Corfu. Works include *The Real Charlotte* (1894) and *Some Experiences of an Irish R.M.* (1899).

1882: Kilmainham Treaty.

Nationalist leader, Charles Stewart Parnell, imprisoned since October 1881, released from jail along with principal lieutenants. Under terms of 'Treaty', Prime Minister Gladstone agreed to deal with thorny question of land arrears and to amend Land Act of 1881.

1923: Dr Patrick Hillery, politician and President of Ireland (1976–90), born at Miltown Malbay, Co. Clare.

1974: In Northern Ireland, six people died and many injured when Loyalists threw bomb into Catholic bar in Belfast.

3/5

1916: Patrick Pearse, educationalist, writer and revolutionary executed in Kilmainham Gaol along with fellow-poet Thomas MacDonagh and Fenian veteran Tom Clarke.

Disappointment with cultural and educational plans had much to do with Pearse's eventual conversion to ranks of Irish Republican Brotherhood. Though appointed Commander-in-Chief of Rising, James Connolly was military leader during days in GPO.

Of his execution, at 3.30 a.m, General Blackader, one of court-martial judges, commented:

> I have just done one of the hardest tasks I have ever had to do. I have had to condemn to death one of the finest characters I have ever come across. There must be something very wrong in the state of things that makes a man like that a rebel.

: Walter Macken, actor, dramatist and novelist, born in Galway. Greatest reputation rests on his historical novels, dealing with Cromwellian invasion, Famine and Easter Rising.

4/5

1773: Art Ó Laoghaire, subject of famous lament *Caoineadh Airt Uí Laoghaire* by his wife, Eibhlín Dhubh Ní Chonaill, killed in encounter with soldiers near Millstreet, Co. Cork.

Ó Laoghaire, formerly captain in Hungarian Hussars under Empress Maria Theresa, met his death after refusing to sell horse for £5 to Abraham Morris, a Protestant. Under statute of William III, no Catholic could own a horse above that value.

Tomb in Kilcrea Abbey bears inscription:
Lo, Arthur Leary, generous, handsome, brave, slain in his bloom,
lies in this humble grave. Died May 4th 1773. Aged 26 years.

1916: Joseph Plunkett, Edward Daly, William Pearse and Michael
O'Hanrahan, executed for participation in Easter Rising.

1941: Second German bombing of Belfast.
Three weeks after first attack (15 April), Luftwaffe returned
and dropped over 90,000 incendiaries across eastern sector of
city. A hundred and fifty killed and similar number seriously
injured.

5/5

1808: Death, aged 26, of Sarah Curran, sweetheart of patriot Robert Emmet, then wife of Captain Henry Sturgeon.

1879: Death of Isaac Butt, barrister, politician and founder of Irish
Home Rule movement (1870).

1916: Execution in Kilmainham Gaol of John MacBride, second-in-
command under Thomas MacDonagh of garrison in Jacob's
factory during Easter Rising.

1953: Death of Robert Lloyd Praeger, botanist and author of *The
Way That I Went* (1937).

1981: Death on sixty-fifth day of his hunger-strike in Long Kesh of
Bobby Sands, MP for Fermanagh and South Tyrone.

6/5

1882: Phoenix Park Murders.
While strolling in Dublin's Phoenix Park, newly arrived
chief-secretary, Lord Frederick Cavendish and under-secretary,
Thomas Burke set upon by six-man gang wielding 12–inch sur-
gical knives – members of 'Invincibles' – and hacked to death.
Burke, in fact, was intended target. Identity of his companion
unknown to assassins. Charles Stewart Parnell and Catholic
Church led chorus of public dismay. As one historian put it,
killings cost Ireland a further generation of slavery.

7/5

1865: Major John MacBride, revolutionary and father of Nobel and Lenin Peace Prize winner Seán MacBride, born in Westport, Co. Mayo.

1915: *Lusitania* disaster.
Cunard Line's 'floating palace' torpedoed by German U-boat off Kinsale, 7 days after leaving New York. Over a thousand perished. Prominent Irish victims included art collector, Sir Hugh Lane and preacher and writer, B.W. Maturin.

1992: Dr Eamonn Casey, RC Bishop of Galway, resigned, and fled country.
Subsequently transpired that he had had secret relationship with American divorcée Annie Murphy, which produced a son.

8/5

1916: Execution of Eamonn Ceannt, Michael Mallin, Con Colbert and Seán Heuston in Kilmainham Gaol for their role in Easter Rising.

1987: In Northern Ireland, eight Provisional IRA members ambushed and shot dead by SAS as they attacked Loughgall RUC Station in Co. Armagh – biggest loss of life sustained by IRA since 1921.

1990: Sudden death in Lourdes of Cardinal Tomás Ó Fiaich, scholar and Archbishop of Armagh since 1977.

9/5

1671: Colonel Thomas Blood attempted to steal crown jewels from Tower of London.
Blood, Irish adventurer who had earlier made two attempts on life of Lord Lieutenant Ormond, arrested in street with crown of England on his person. Subsequently brought to trial, insisted on being heard by King Charles II who pardoned him and awarded him annual pension of £500.

1828: Charles J. Kickham, novelist and Fenian, born at Mullinahone, Co. Tipperary. Works include *Knocknagow* (1879).

1896: Austin Clarke, poet, novelist and dramatist, born in Dublin. Many volumes include *Flight to Africa* (1963) and *Mnemosyne Lay in the Dust* (1966).

1916: Thomas Kent, revolutionary, executed at Cork military detention barracks.

10/5

1886: General Richard 'Dick' Mulcahy, soldier and politician, born in Waterford.

1925: Death in office in Wellington of William Ferguson Massey, Prime Minister of New Zealand since 1912.

1943: Nineteen men killed when 500-pound mine exploded without warning at Ballymanus Bay, Co. Donegal.

11/5

1745: Battle of Fontenoy, scene of Marshal de Saxe's French victory over British and Allied forces during War of the Austrian Succession.

Comment about Irishmen 'fighting every nation's battles save their own' usually refers to celebrated Irish Brigade which fought for a century under flag of France. Brigade formed from ranks of a 5,000-strong force of Irish soldiers under Lord Mountcashel was dispatched to France in 1690 as part of a deal by which James II granted similar number of French infantry. Following Treaty of Limerick, joined by further eleven thousand Jacobite soldiers – so-called 'Wild Geese' – and for century afterwards regularly reinforced by thousands of other exiles. Price of service was high. Estimated that between 1692 and 1792, year brigade was disbanded, roughly half-a-million Irishmen died in service of France.

Though rendering distinguished service on such famous battlefields as Blenheim, Ramillies, Oudenarde and Malplaquet, brigade's crowning moment at Fontenoy where, under Lord Clare, charged enemy to turn imminent defeat into total victory.

1788: Dr Henry Cooke, Presbyterian leader renowned as 'framer

of sectarianism in the politics of Ulster' born at Grillagh, Co.
Derry.

1971: Death of Seán Lemass, founder member of Fianna Fáil and
Taoiseach (1959–66).

12/5

1751: Archibald Hamilton Rowan, United Irishman, born in London.

1916: James Connolly and Seán MacDiarmada executed in Kilmainham Gaol for their part in Easter Rising.

1944: Death in Nairobi, Kenya, aged 36, of Edel Mary Quinn,
Legion of Mary envoy to Africa.

13/5

1919: During War of Independence, two policemen killed on train
at Knocklong Station, Co. Limerick when IRA man Seán
Hogan rescued from police custody by comrades – Dan
Breen and Seán Treacy.

1986: Death of Peadar O'Donnell, socialist, Republican, revolutionary and novelist. Works include *Islanders* (1928), *The
Big Window* (1955) and *There Will be Another Day* (1963).

14/5

1734: Death of Richard Cantillon, economist.
Cantillon, born at Ballyheige, Co. Kerry in 1680, has been
called 'father of political economy' on account of one famous
book, *Essai sur la nature du commerce en général, traduit de
l'Anglais* (1755). Murdered by his cook who ransacked and set
fire to his London home before making good his escape.

1784: Irish Post Office established by statute.

15/5

1808: Michael William Balfe, violinist, singer and composer, born in Dublin.

1847: Death in Genoa, while on his way to Rome, of Daniel O'Connell, 'The Liberator'.
Last appearance in House of Commons, in January 1847, described thus by a contemporary:

> In a speech of simple and touching eloquence, delivered in great physical pain and agony of mind, he pleaded for relief for the starving people. That he was himself face to face with death was only too evident. His voice was so faint that few could catch his words, although he spoke from the Treasury Bench, by courtesy of the House, to enable his speech to be better heard. He was listened to with a respectful – even a reverential – silence, and statesmen of all parties testified their sympathy by their subsequent inquiries about his health, and a message of sympathy was conveyed to him by the sovereign.

1867: Eoin MacNeill, scholar and patriot, born in Glenarm, Co. Antrim.

1971: Death of Sir Tyrone Guthrie, theatre producer whose home, Annaghmakerrig House, Newbliss, Co. Monaghan, serves as retreat for artists and writers.

16/5
Feast of St Brendan ('Brendan the Navigator')

1926: Fianna Fáil ('Soldiers of Destiny'), subtitled 'The Republican Party', founded by Eamon De Valera.
Aims were reunification of Ireland, preservation of Irish language, distribution of large farms among small farmers and policy of protection and self-sufficiency for Irish economy.

1945: De Valera's reply to Churchill.
Famous speech made on Radió Éireann 3 days after Churchill's stinging attack on him personally and Irish neutrality during victory address on BBC:

Mr Churchill is proud of Britain's stand alone after France had fallen and before America entered the war. Could he not find in his heart the generosity to acknowledge that there is a small nation that stood alone, not for one year or two, but for several hundred years against aggression; that endured spoliations, famines, massacres, in endless succession; that was clubbed many times into insensibility but each time on regaining consciousness, took up the fight anew; a small nation that could never be got to accept defeat and has never surrendered her soul?

17/5

1599: 'The Pass of the Plumes', Co. Laois.

Detachment of army of Lord Lieutenant Robert Devereux, set upon by Owney O'More of Laois. Place, near village of Timahoe became known as 'The Pass of the Plumes' on account of number of plumes from English helmets left on ground. Some five hundred English soldiers killed.

1974: Loyalist bombs exploded without warning in Dublin and Monaghan town.

Twenty-five people killed and over a hundred injured in Dublin; six died in Monaghan.

18/5

1928: Death of Standish James O'Grady, historian and novelist. Works include *Early Bardic Literature of Ireland* (1879), *Finn and his Companions* (1892) and *The Triumph and Passion of Cuchulain* (1919).

1939: First aircraft landed at Rineanna, now Shannon Airport.

Irish Air Corps Auro-Ansen Mark 1 Serial 43 touched down at 1.27 p.m. after one-hour flight from Baldonnel, Co. Dublin.

1983: Death of Frank Aiken, IRA leader, Dáil deputy for Co. Louth for over 50 years and minister in every Fianna Fáil government from 1932 to 1973.

19/5

1798: Arrest of Lord Edward FitzGerald, United Irishman.

Lord Edward, 'on the run' with £1,000 on his head, seized in house in Thomas Street, Dublin, by troops under Major Sirr. In fierce struggle, Lord Edward killed one of arresting party and was himself shot in arm. Died from wounds 16 days later.

1832: Standish Hayes O'Grady, engineer, Gaelic scholar and cousin of Standish James O'Grady, born at Castleconnell, Co. Limerick.

20/5

1790: Death of Elizabeth Gunning, Duchess of Hamilton and Argyll.

Elizabeth, and her older sister, Maria, daughters of John Gunning of Castlecoote, Co. Roscommon, were celebrated beauties. Maria, who married Earl of Coventry, died in her late twenties, apparently from ill-effects of using white lead paint as a cosmetic. Elizabeth, who was twice married, to Dukes of Hamilton and of Argyll, died in her late fifties. In words of a contemporary, 'She seemed composed of a finer clay than the rest of her sex'.

1932: First transatlantic solo flight by a women pilot.

Amelia Earhart landed at Culmore, Co. Derry, having flown from Harbour Grace, Newfoundland – a distance of 2,206 miles – in 13 hours.

1977: Death of Harry Brogan, actor and leading figure in modern Irish theatre.

21/5

1910: Death in Brisbane, Australia of Mary Anne Kelly, poet, 'Eva of *The Nation*'.

Born in Headford, Co. Galway, was wife of Young Irelander and medical doctor Kevin Izod O'Doherty (1823–1905).

1921: Northern Ireland's first general election.

Unionists won 40 seats, Nationalists 6 seats and Sinn Féin 6 seats. Nationalist and Sinn Féin MPs declined to take seats in Stormont Parliament.

1944: Mary Robinson, lawyer and seventh President of Ireland (1990–), born in Ballina, Co. Mayo.

22/5

1807: Death of Henry Essex Edgeworth, confessor to Madame Elizabeth of France.

Born at Mostrim or Edgeworthstown, Co. Longford in 1745, was ordained in Paris in 1769 under name 'de Firmont' and subsequently appointed spiritual director to Madame Elizabeth, sister of King Louis XVI. In January 1793, Louis asked for Abbé de Firmont who heard his confession and escorted him to guillotine. Spent later years as chaplain-cum-diplomat to exiled Bourbons.

1849: Death of Maria Edgeworth, writer.

Daughter of landlord and inventor Richard Lovell Edgeworth, was author of *Castle Rackrent* (1800) and a string of similar novels on Irish life. Though 'courted by all persons of distinction', she died a spinster.

1932: Death of Lady Augusta Gregory, playwright, folklorist and co-founder of Abbey Theatre.

1972: Death of Cecil Day-Lewis, poet, critic, novelist, English poet laureate (1968) and father of actor Daniel Day-Lewis.

23/5

1754: William Drennan, medical doctor, United Irishman, poet and writer, born in Belfast, son of a Presbyterian minister.

Originator of Society of the United Irishmen but played no part in activities of Society after 1794 when he was tried and acquitted on charge of sedition. Thereafter, settled in Belfast where he founded Belfast Academical Institution and *Belfast Magazine*. Wrote great deal of popular poetry, notably 'Memories of William Orr' or 'The Wake of William Orr'. First to apply to Ireland epithet, 'emerald isle'.

1798: Rising ('98 Rebellion) broke out, as planned, in Leinster.

Insurgents repulsed at Naas and Clane and defeated at Rathangan – North Cork militia massacred at Prosperous.

24/5

1487: 10-year-old Lambert Simnel, alleged nephew of King Edward V of York, crowned as Edward VI in Christ Church Cathedral, Dublin.

1923: Irish Civil War ended with ceasefire.
Began in earnest in June 1922 with Free State bombardment of Republican garrison in Four Courts; claimed combined pro- and anti-Treaty losses of approximately three hundred lives per month or just under four thousand in all. During struggle, seventy-seven Republicans executed by Free State authorities.

1923: Siobhán McKenna, leading lady of modern Irish theatre, born in Belfast.

25/5

1842: Helen Blackburn, pioneer suffragette, born on Valentia Island, Co. Kerry.
Was in vanguard of Britain's women's movement. In 1902, a year before her death, published *Women's Suffrage: a Record of the Movement in the British Isles*, for many years the standard work on the subject.

1885: Gerald Boland, founder member of Fianna Fáil and government minister, born in Manchester.

1921: War of Independence: Custom House in Dublin burned down by IRA.

26/5

1868: Execution, outside Newgate prison in London of Michael Barrett, Fenian – last public execution in British Isles.
Had been convicted of participation in Clerkenwell prison explosion of December 1867. Public executions abolished under terms of the Capital Punishment Amendment Act which came into force three days later.

1977: Five soldiers killed by shrapnel in training accident on Irish army's artillery range in Glen of Imaal, Co. Wicklow.

27/5

1798: Battle of Oulart Hill, Co. Wexford, in which insurgents under Fr John Murphy defeated North Cork militia and yeomanry.

1936: Aer Lingus, known then as Irish Sea Airways, inaugurated its first route from Baldonnel military aerodrome to Bristol.
The *Iolar* (Eagle), a De Havilland Dragon, the airline's sole aircraft, carried full complement of five passengers.

28/5

1779: Thomas Moore, poet, born in Dublin, son of a grocer and wine merchant. As well as *Irish Melodies*, wrote lives of Byron, Sheridan and Lord Edward FitzGerald.

1929: Death of Alice Stopford Green, historian. Author of *The Making of Ireland and its Undoing* (1908) and *Irish Nationality* (1911).

1974: In Northern Ireland, collapse, after Loyalist strike, of power-sharing executive, set up on 1 January, in wake of Sunningdale Agreement.

29/5

1884: Oscar Wilde married Constance Mary Lloyd.
Constance, born in Wexford, first met Wilde in London, in 1881, and immediately fell in love with the aspiring playwright. 'I can't help liking him,' she wrote, 'because when he's talking to me alone he's never a bit affected'. Wilde, for his part, described her as 'a grave slight violet-eyed little Artemis with great coils of heavy brown hair which make her head droop like a blossom'.

1896: Irish Socialist Republican Party founded by James Connolly.

30/5

1784: St Mary's in Chapel Lane – Belfast's first Catholic Church – was opened for public worship.
Opened at a time when Belfast's Catholics numbered

thirteen hundred out of total population of fifteen thousand. Local Presbyterians subscribed £84 towards total cost of £170. Vicar of Belfast, the Rev. William Bristow, donated gilt mahogany pulpit, still preserved in now restored building.

1986: Connaught Regional Airport, Knock, Co. Mayo officially opened by Fianna Fáil leader, Charles J. Haughey.

31/5

1744: Richard Lovell Edgeworth, landlord, inventor and father of writer Maria Edgeworth, born in Bath, England.

Inventions included a velocipede, a pedometer, and a semaphore which transmitted messages from Dublin to Galway in 8 minutes. Was married four times and fathered twenty-two children, nineteen surviving infancy. 'I am not,' he said, 'a man of prejudices. I have had four wives. The second and third were sisters, and I was in love with the second in the lifetime of the first.'

1847: Alice Stopford Green, historian, born in Kells, Co. Meath. Works include *A History of the Irish State to 1014* (1925).

1906: Death of Michael Davitt, founder of Irish National Land League (1879).

1941: North Strand Bombings, Dublin.

500-pound German bomb landed in North Strand area of Dublin, killing over thirty people, injuring ninety and leaving over five hundred homeless. Smaller bomb damaged Áras an Uachtaráin and American Embassy. In 1958, German government paid £327,000 compensation.

June

1/6

1762: Edmund Ignatius Rice, founder of Irish Christian Brothers, born at Westcourt, Callan, Co. Kilkenny.

1852: Submarine telegraph cable between Holyhead and Howth linked Britain and Ireland for first time.

1866: Fenian 'Invasion' of Canada.

Fenian force of US Civil War veterans, numbering eight hundred and led by Monaghan-born Col. John O'Neill, crossed Niagara river from Buffalo, New York and raised the green flag on Canadian soil. Following day, at Ridgeway, Ontario, routed Queen's militia sent by rail from Toronto to repel them. On 3 June, withdrew across Lake Erie where they were arrested by General Meade on board *USS Michigan*.

1984: US President Ronald Reagan and his wife, Nancy, arrived in Ireland on 4-day official visit.

During his stay, President conferred with honorary Doctor of Laws degree at University College, Galway; addressed joint session of Oireachtas and visited his ancestral birthplace, Bally-poreen, Co. Tipperary, from where great-grandfather, Michael Reagan, emigrated to America in 1858.

2/6

1567: Shane O'Neill, Ulster chieftain known as 'Seán an Díomais'

('Shane the Proud'), murdered by MacDonnells, at Cushendun, Co. Antrim.

1829: Death, aged 90, of Lady Eleanor Butler, recluse of Llangollen.

A daughter of sixteenth Earl of Ormond, lived for over 50 years with friend, Sarah Ponsonby, in cottage at Plasnewyyd in Vale of Llangollen. Neither left cottage for single night until death.

Described by Prince Puckler-Muskace as 'the two most celebrated virgins of Europe', 'the Ladies of Llangollen', who usually dressed in semi-masculine attire, attracted numerous visitors to vale including notables from world of fashion and literature. Duke of Wellington procured for them pension of £200 a year.

1954: Fifteenth Dáil Éireann assembled.

John A. Costello (Fine Gael) became Taoiseach in coalition government.

3/6
Feast of St Kevin of Glendalough

1836: Death of Barry O'Meara, surgeon to Napoleon Bonaparte.

Born Churchtown, Mallow, Co. Cork, accompanied Napoleon to St Helena in 1815, as personal physician. Both he and ex-emperor in constant loggerheads with governor of island, Sir Hudson Lowe, native of Galway. 1818, Lowe dismissed O'Meara for refusing to report Napoleon's private conversations.

In 1822, year after Napoleon's death, O'Meara denounced Lowe's treatment of Napoleon in *Napoleon in Exile: or a voice from St Helena*. Book caused sensation and led to Lowe spending last years of his life – died in 1844 – in fruitless campaign to clear his reputation.

1878: Sinéad De Valera, wife of Eamon De Valera, born Sinéad Flanagan in Balbriggan, Co. Dublin.

4/6
1798: Death at Newgate prison of 34-year-old Lord Edward

FitzGerald, United Irishman.

1820: Death of Henry Grattan, patriot and orator.

1849: Death of Marguerite (née Power), Countess of Blessington, novelist, beauty and gossip writer. Works include *Conversations with Lord Byron* (1834).

1886: Belfast riots (until September).
As Home Rule Bill being debated in House of Commons, sectarian scuffle broke out between group of navvies working at docks. Trouble spread throughout city leading to three months of most serious sectarian rioting of century.

5/6

1646: Battle of Benburb (Co. Tyrone), in which forces of Owen Roe O'Neill inflicted crushing defeat on English-Scotch parliamentarians under Robert Monroe.

1798: Battle of New Ross, Co. Wexford, in which insurgents under Bagenal Harvey were routed.
Between one and two hundred Protestant prisoners massacred at Scullabogue, Co. Wexford.

1868: James Connolly, socialist and one of seven signatories of 1916 Proclamation of the Irish Republic, born of Irish immigrant parents in Edinburgh.

1899: Death of Margaret Anne Cusack, the 'Nun of Kenmare'.
Margaret Anne Cusack, in religion Sister Mary Frances Clare, variously described as the 'Joan of Arc of Ireland' and 'Ireland's first suffragette' on account of hostility endured at hands of Catholic hierarchy, and radical views on rôle of women in society. Eventually left Catholic Church and died – as she was born – a Protestant.

1916: Lord Kitchener, field marshal, lost at sea when *HMS Hampshire* struck a mine off the Orkneys.

1920: Cornelius Ryan, war-correspondent and bestselling author, born in Dublin. Works include *The Longest Day* (1959) and *The Last Battle* (1960).

6/6

1880: W.T. (William Thomas) Cosgrave, first President of the Executive Council of the Irish Free State (1922–32), born in Dublin.

1898: Ninette De Valois, founder of London's Sadler's Wells ballet school, born in Wicklow.

1941: Death of John Hughes, sculptor.
Best known works include 'Man of Sorrows' and 'Madonna and Child' for Loughrea Cathedral, Co. Galway; a monument of Charles J. Kickham in Tipperary and the Gladstone monument in Hawarden.

7/6

1798: Battle of Antrim, in which insurgents under Henry Joy McCracken defeated by Crown forces.

1892: Kevin O'Higgins, politician and minister in first Free State government, born at Stradbally, Co. Laois.

1925: Death of Matt Talbot, the 'Servant of God'.
Dublin labourer, devout Catholic who lived frugally and practised self-mortification. After his death it was discovered that he wore chains on waist, arm and leg. October 1976, Catholic Church gave him title of 'Venerable'.

8/6

1859: *The Irish Times* became daily newspaper.
In first leading article, 23-year-old founder and editor Major Lawrence Knox wrote: 'Our intention, in short, is to make *The Irish Times* a first rate Irish newspaper, complete in its details, sagacious and consistent in its policy, and faithfully reflecting the opinions of the most independent, intelligent and truly progressive portion of Irish society'.

1985: In sport, Barry McGuigan, known as 'The Clones Cyclone' defeated Eusebio Pedroza to win world featherweight boxing title.

9/6
Feast of St Colmcille or Columba

1798: Battle of Arklow, Co. Wicklow, in which insurgents led by Fr Michael Murphy (killed in action) were defeated.

1888: Sir Basil Brooke, Viscount Brookeborough, Prime Minister of Northern Ireland (1943–63), born at Colebrook, Co. Fermanagh.

10/6
1944: Death in sanatorium in Dresden of Frank Ryan, Republican and socialist.
    Born near Elton, Co. Limerick, helped to organise radical Saor Éire movement in 1931. 1936, led contingent of two hundred Irishmen to Spain to fight in International Brigade for the Republic against Franco. Subsequently imprisoned, spent last years in Germany where he was treated as a non-party neutral.

11/6
1862: Violet Florence Martin, novelist under pen-name 'Martin Ross' and literary partner of her cousin, Edith Somerville, born at Ross House, Co. Galway. Works include *The Real Charlotte* (1894) and *Dan Russell the Fox* (1911).

1925: Speech by W.B. Yeats in Seanad Éireann debate on divorce:

> If you show that this country, Southern Ireland, is going to be governed by Catholic ideas and by Catholic ideas alone, you will never get the North ... You will put a wedge into the midst of this nation ... You are now going to act on the advice of men who do not express the poetical mind, but who express the religious mind ... In the long warfare of this country with England the Catholic clergy took the side of the people, and owing to that they possess here an influence that they do not possess anywhere else in Europe ... I am proud to consider myself a typical man of that minority. We, against whom you have done this thing, are no petty people.

We are one of the great stocks of Europe. We are the people of Burke; we are the people of Grattan; we are the people of Swift, the people of Emmet, the people of Parnell. We have created the most of the modern literature of this country. We have created the best of its political intelligence. Yet I do not altogether regret what has happened....

12/6

1786: George Robert Fitzgerald, notorious rogue, known as 'Fighting Fitzgerald', hanged at Castlebar, Co. Mayo.

1889: Armagh Railway Disaster.
    In 2-train collision during annual Armagh–Warrenpoint excursion of Armagh Methodist Sunday School, eighty died and almost four hundred were injured. Worst disaster in Irish railway history.

1973: In Northern Ireland, six people, all elderly, died in Provisional IRA car-bomb in Coleraine, Co. Derry.

13/6

1699: Funeral took place of 29-year-old Molly Malone, Dublin fishmonger and subject of famous ballad.

1798: Battle of Ballynahinch, Co. Down.
    Seven-thousand-strong insurgent army led by General Henry Munro defeated by Crown force of two thousand under General Nugent. Ballynahinch and surrounding area subsequently pillaged and looted by troops. Amongst victims was legendary Betsy Gray, shot and mutilated along with her brother George and lover Willie Boal. Munro was betrayed and later hanged and beheaded opposite his home in Lisburn. Ballynahinch marked end of the Rising in Ulster.

1865: William Butler Yeats, poet, dramatist, co-founder of Abbey Theatre (1904) and winner of Nobel Prize for Literature (1923), born at Sandymount Avenue, Dublin, eldest son of painter, John Butler Yeats.

1951: Fourteenth Dáil Éireann assembled.
    Fianna Fáil, under Eamon De Valera, returned to office, with

support of independents. Remained in office until May 1954.

1990: Death of Captain Terence O'Neill, Prime Minister of Northern Ireland (1963–9).

14/6

1690: William III landed at Carrickfergus, Co. Antrim.
Former Prince of Orange arrived with thirty-six-thousand-strong army, mainly foreign mercenaries, Danes, Germans and Huguenots.

1884: John McCormack, operatic and concert tenor, born at Athlone, Co. Westmeath, of Scottish parents.
In every sense an all-rounder, as much at home singing German *Lieder*, Italian and French operas and oratorios as with sacred music and popular ballads. Though fluent in French, German and Italian, failed to master Irish language and was reluctant to perform in it.

15/6

1828: Sir Thomas Newenham Deane, architect of Dublin's National Library and Museum, born at Dundanion, Co. Cork.

1848: Death of Thomas Steele, landlord.
Born at Derrymore, Co. Clare and known as 'Honest Tom Steele' on account of sincerity. Protestant who spent fortune in support of Catholic Emancipation and Repeal of Union. Devastated by O'Connell's death a year earlier, attempted suicide by throwing himself into Thames from Waterloo Bridge. Though rescued, died a few days later. Buried beside O'Connell in Glasnevin cemetery.

1891: Death, aged 91, of Charles James Patrick Mahon, the O'Gorman Mahon, politician, soldier and last of Irish daredevils.
Extraordinary career. After period as lieutenant in Tsar of Russia's international bodyguard, travelled to China and India and fought under Turkish and Austrian flags. 1860s, progressed to South America, served as general in Uruguay, held rank of admiral in Chilean navy, was appointed colonel by Emperor of Brazil and took part in American Civil War on side of the Union. It was he who introduced Captain O'Shea to Parnell.

1919: First non-stop transatlantic flight.

  John W. Alcock and Arthur Whitten Brown in a Vickers
Vimy biplane landed near Clifden, Co. Galway, having flown
from Newfoundland in 15 hours, 57 minutes.

1988: In Northern Ireland, six British soldiers killed by Provisional IRA bomb planted under minibus in Lisburn, Co. Antrim.

16/6

1864: Death of William Smith O'Brien, Nationalist and Young Ireland leader.

1904: 'Bloomsday'.

  James Joyce first walked out with Nora Barnacle in tribute to
whom he set his internationally acclaimed *Ulysses* on that date.

17/6

1349: Last entry in annals of Friar John Clyn.

  Great Plague or 'Black Death' which swept across Europe in
mid-fourteenth century reached east coast of Ireland in autumn
1348. Within a few weeks both Drogheda, its probable port of
entry, and Dublin were almost entirely wiped out.

  Impossible to say how many died as a result, though losses
were so great that many believed end of world was nigh. Franciscan annalist John Clyn, himself a victim of plague, voiced
this fear in last entry in his annals:

> Seeing these many ills and how the whole world is, as it
> were, in an ill plight, among the dead expecting death's
> coming, I have set them down in writing, truthfully as I have
> heard them and tested them; and lest the writing should
> perish with the writer and the work fail with the worker, I
> leave parchment to carry on the work, if perchance any may
> survive or any of the race of Adam may be able to escape
> this pestilence and continue the work I have begun.

1867: John Robert Gregg, inventor of Gregg Shorthand, born at
Rockcorry, Co. Monaghan.

18/6

1769: Robert Stewart, Lord Castlereagh, born in Dublin.

Achieved notoriety by securing passage of Act of Union, through mixture of persuasion, bribery and intimidation.

When, in July 1800, Irish parliament voted itself out of existence, an eyewitness recorded:

> The Bill received the Royal assent without a muttering, or a whispering, or a protesting echo of a sigh ... One person only I remarked whose features were suddenly illuminated by a smile, a sarcastic smile as I read it. It was Lord Castlereagh.

1815: Battle of Waterloo, scene of Napoleon's defeat by troops of Wellington and Blücher.

Duke of Wellington was Irish – though disliked being told so – and many Irishmen of all ranks fought under him. Inniskilling Dragoons took part in famous charge downhill which drove back first major French infantry attack under d'Erlon.

On French side, there were Irishmen too, though not in significant numbers. Marshal Ney, who acted as fighting commander while Napoleon sat behind, was of Irish descent, and was even red-headed. If impetuosity really is an Irish characteristic, Ney certainly had it. His impatience and propensity for hand-to-hand fighting were potent factors in his side's defeat.

1901: Denis Johnston, actor and dramatist, born in Dublin. Works include *The Old Lady Says No* (1929) and *The Moon on the Yellow River* (1931).

1992: Referendum on Maastricht Treaty on European Union (Yes 69.1%; No 30.9%).

19/6

1892: Sermon by Parish Priest, Roundwood, Co. Wicklow:

> Parnellism is a simple love of adultery and all those who profess Parnellism profess to love and admire adultery. They are an adulterous set, their leaders are open and avowed adulterers, and therefore I say to you, as parish priest, beware of these Parnellites when they enter your house, you that have wives and daughters, for they will do all they can to commit these adulteries, for their cause is not patriotism – it is adultery – and they back Parnellism because it gratifies their adultery.

1928: Death of Donn Byrne, US born novelist. Works include *Destiny Bay* (1928) and *The Golden Coat* (1930)

20/6

1584: Torture and execution of Dermot O'Hurley, RC Archbishop of Cashel since 1581.

Born at Lycadoon, Co. Limerick, suspected of conspiring between Catholic powers in Europe and rebel forces opposed to Crown rule in Ireland. For almost two years, administered his diocese 'vainly sought after by the English but protected by the care and devotion of the Irish, disguising his identity by wearing secular dress'. According to one version of events, he was eventually discovered while sheltering at Slane Castle.

1763: Theobald Wolfe Tone, United Irishman, born in Dublin.

1849: Death of malnutrition in Dublin of 46-year-old James Clarence Mangan, poet, renowned for haunting translation of sixteenth-century 'Róisín Dubh' (Dark Rosaleen).

1891: John A. Costello, lawyer and Taoiseach in first two coalition governments (1948–51), (1954–7), born in Dublin.

21/6

1798: Battle of Vinegar Hill, Enniscorthy, Co. Wexford, in which local insurgents defeated by Crown forces under General Lake. Lake's victory effectively ended Rising in Wexford.

1854: 20-year-old David Lucas threw unexploded Russian bomb over side of *HMS Hecla*, on board which he was serving during Crimean War.

Cited for his bravery, he subsequently – June 1857 – became the first recipient of the Victoria Cross.

1958: Death of Alexander Brenon, film director.

Born in Dún Laoghaire, Co. Dublin, directed some 300 films, including first version of *Beau Geste* (1926).

22/6

1921: King George V opened Northern Ireland Parliament at Stormont with impassioned plea for peace in Ireland.

1922: Assassination outside his home in London of Field Marshal Sir Henry Wilson.

Had been official adviser to Stormont Minister of Home Affairs on organisation and control of Special Constabulary. Two members of London battalion of IRA, Reginald Dunne and Joseph O'Sullivan, later hanged for his murder.

1932: Thirty-first International Eucharistic Congress opened in Dublin.

1965: Death of Piaras Béaslaí (Pierce Beasley), Liverpool-born revolutionary and writer, mainly in the Irish language. Works include *Fear na Milliún Púnt* (1915) and *Bealtaine 1916 agus Dánta Eile* (1920).

1968: Death of Captain Patrick J. Saul, pioneer aviator.

Navigator for Sir Charles Kingsford-Smith aboard *Southern Cross* on historic east–west transatlantic flight from Portmarnock, Co. Dublin to Newfoundland.

23/6

1775: William Brown, admiral in Argentinian navy, born in Foxford, Co. Mayo.

1802: Daniel O'Connell, 'The Liberator' secretly married his cousin, Mary O'Connell.

I said, 'Miss O'Connell [she was also an O'Connell], are you engaged?' She replied, 'I am not'. I said, 'Then will you engage yourself to me?' 'I will', was her reply; and I said I would devote my life to make her happy. She deserved that I should. She gave me 34 years of the purest happiness that man ever enjoyed.

Daniel O'Connell on death of his wife, October 1836.

1959: Seán Lemass became Taoiseach and leader of Fianna Fáil.

24/6

1797: Most Rev. John Hughes, first Archbishop of New York

(1850), born at Annaloghlan, Co. Tyrone.

1834: Kerry faction fight.
In one of bloodiest faction-fights of nineteenth century, Cooleens and Lawlor-Black Mulvihills clashed at Ballyveigh Strand, Co. Kerry. Over two hundred were killed and several hundred injured.

1850: Lord Kitchener, celebrated British field marshal, born at Ballylongford, Co. Kerry.

1966: Death of Patrick 'Paddy the Cope' Gallagher, founder of Templecrone Co-Operative Society (1906).

25/6

1731: The Dublin Society, later Royal Dublin Society (RDS) founded by group of landlords and Church of Ireland clergy with object of 'improving husbandry, manufactures and other useful arts and sciences'.

1870: Robert Erskine Childers, patriot and author, born in London. Works include *The Riddle of the Sands* (1903).

1876: Battle of Little Big Horn, Montana, USA.
Of General George Armstrong Custer's total command of six hundred and four men, a hundred and seventy-one born in Ireland, including half of two hundred and seventy-three soldiers killed that fateful day. Seven of these Irish immigrants awarded Congressional Medal of Honour, America's highest military honour. Lone survivor of massacre, cavalry horse 'Commanche', owned by Captain Myles Walter Keogh from Carlow.

1891: Charles Stewart Parnell, Nationalist leader, married Katharine O'Shea at Steyning, near Brighton.

1919: Death of William Martin Murphy, founder of Independent Newspapers.

1938: Douglas Hyde installed as first President of Ireland.

1945: Seán T. Ó Ceallaigh installed as second President of Ireland.

1950: 46-year-old Gaelic writer Muiris Ó Súilleabháin drowned while bathing in Co. Galway. Works include *Fiche Bliain Ag Fás/Twenty Years A-Growing* (1933).

1959: Eamon De Valera installed as third President of Ireland.

1973: Erskine Hamilton Childers, son of Robert Erskine Childers, installed as fourth President of Ireland.

26/6

1824: William Thomson Kelvin, Lord Kelvin, scientist and inventor, born in Belfast.

1848: Francis Rawdon Crozier, explorer, disappeared in Arctic.
      Born in Banbridge, Co. Down, commanded *Terror* on Sir John Franklin's expedition to Arctic which sailed from England in 1845. Fate unknown until record of expedition discovered in cairn near Cape Herscel by another Irish explorer, Captain Leopold McClintock. According to document, both ships of expedition had been beset by ice off King William's Island in September 1846. Franklin had died in June 1847 and both ships been abandoned in April 1848. Document concluded stating that Crozier and remaining hundred survivors were 'to set out tomorrow, June 26 1848 for Back's Fish River'. None ever again seen alive.

1963: US President John Fitzgerald Kennedy and his wife, Jackie, arrived in Ireland on 4-day official visit.
      First US President to visit Ireland, was conferred with honorary degree by Trinity College, Dublin; addressed joint session of Oireachtas; received Freedom of cities of Dublin, Cork, Galway and Limerick and visited his ancestral homestead at Dunganstown, Co. Wexford.

1981: Twenty-second Dáil Éireann assembled.
      Garret FitzGerald elected Taoiseach in Fine Gael–Labour coalition.

27/6

1846: Charles Stewart Parnell, Nationalist leader, born at Avondale, Co. Wicklow.

Though John Henry Parnell, who died when Charles was 13, was sympathetic to Nationalist cause, Parnell's mother generally credited with nurturing his patriotism. Of Scots-Irish Presbyterian stock, Delia Tudor Stewart Parnell was a daughter of Admiral Charles 'Old Ironside' Stewart whose exploits included capture of two British ships during Anglo–American conflict of 1812.

In 17 turbulent years in politics, Parnell brought together, for first time in Irish history, three powerful forces – constitutionalism, physical force nationalism and agrarianism – and skilfully maintained balance of power between all three.

28/6

1844: John Boyle O'Reilly, writer, and in his day most respected Irish voice in United States, born at Dowth Castle, Co. Meath. Works include *Songs from the Southern Seas* (1873) and *Moondyne* (1880).

1861: Death of Robert O'Hara Burke, explorer of Australia.

Born in Co. Galway, emigrated to Australia in 1853 and became Inspector of Police in Victoria. 1860, given charge of expedition to cross Australian continent from south to north. February 1861, he and three companions, Wills, Gray and King reached tidal waters of Flinders River to become first white men to cross continent. On return journey, Gray, Wills and Burke died of starvation. Sole survivor, John King, cared for by aborigines. Remains of Burke and Wills interred in Melbourne where a monument in city centre erected in their honour.

1912: Irish Labour Party founded in Clonmel, Co. Tipperary when Irish Trades Union Congress (ITUC) constituted itself 'Irish Trades Union Congress and Labour Party'.

29/6

1819: The Colleen Bawn murder case.

16-year-old Ellen Hanley, the so-called 'Colleen Bawn', went missing from her home in Co. Limerick. Three months later, body washed ashore at Moneypoint on Shannon, bearing unmistakable evidence that she had been murdered.

John Scanlan, young squire from one of leading families of the county, subsequently convicted and hanged for her murder.

His batman, Stephen Sullivan, who vanished after the murder, later discovered and convicted.

Story inspired Gerald Griffin's *The Collegians* (1829), Dion Boucicault's play *The Colleen Bawn* (1860) and Benedict's opera *The Lily of Killarney.*

1842: Maurice Davin, athlete and first President of GAA, born in Carrick-on-Suir, Co. Tipperary.

30/6

1915: Death in New York of Jeremiah O'Donovan Rossa, Nationalist.

1922: Conclusion of Siege of Four Courts, which marked start of Civil War.

After 3 days of bombardment by forces of Provisional Government using battery of 4 18-pound field guns borrowed from British, Republican garrison of two hundred surrendered. Same day, Public Record Office, part of Four Courts complex, blown up, causing destruction of national archives dating back to 1174.

July

1681: Oliver Plunkett, Archbishop of Armagh, hanged, drawn and quartered at Tyburn – last Catholic martyred there.

1690: Battle of the Boyne, Co. Meath.
William of Orange, with army of some thirty-six thousand men, including English, Scots, Danes, Germans and Huguenots, met James II with army mainly of French and Irish, numbering about twenty-five thousand. William's victory, despite gallantry of Irish cavalry, led to James' flight and opened way to Dublin.

1867: Thomas Francis Meagher, Nationalist known as 'Meagher of the Sword' and brigadier-general of Irish Brigade which fought for Union in American Civil War, drowned in mysterious circumstances in Missouri river.

1916: Battle of the Somme, northern France, began.
In first two days of battle, three thousand men of 36th (Ulster) Division killed and a further two thousand, five hundred injured – one of bloodiest episodes of First World War.

1990: Reception for Republic of Ireland's World Cup team.
Estimated five hundred thousand people took to streets of Dublin to welcome team on their return from Italy. Republic of Ireland team, in first appearance in the competition, beaten in semi-finals by host nation.

1970: Irish Catholic hierarchy announced that it was no longer obligatory to abstain from eating meat on Fridays.

1980: Death of General Tom Barry, Republican soldier and guerrilla tactician renowned for successes against Crown forces at Kilmichael and Crossbarry, Co. Cork during War of Independence.

1990: Nelson Mandela, Deputy President of African National Congress, addressed Dáil Éireann.

3/7
1746: Henry Grattan, patriot and orator, born in Dublin.

1816: Death of Dorothy Jordan, actress and mistress of Duke of Clarence, later William IV, by whom she bore five sons and five daughters.

4/7
American Independence Day (1776)
From beginning of eighteenth century, an estimated quarter of a million 'Scotch Irish' – lowland Scots, mainly Presbyterians who had settled in Ulster a century earlier – emigrated to New World; 'a grim, stern people, strong and simple, powerful for good or evil', in words of Theodore Roosevelt whose mother came from Larne, Co. Antrim. They were the men who made America, becoming her soldiers, inventors, railroad chiefs, bankers, politicians, and presidents.
 US Presidents of Scotch-Irish descent:
 Andrew Jackson, seventh President (1829–37)
 James Knox Polk, eleventh President (1845–9)
 James Buchanan, fifteenth President (1857–61)
 Andrew Johnson, seventeenth President (1865–9)
 Ulysses Simpson Grant, eighteenth President (1869–77)
 Chester Alan Arthur, twenty-first President (1881–5)
 Grover Cleveland, twenty-second and twenty-fourth President (1885–9 and 1893–7)
 Benjamin Harrison, twenty-third President (1889–93)
 William McKinley, twenty-fifth President (1897–1901)
 Theodore Roosevelt, twenty-sixth President (1901–9)
 Woodrow Wilson, twenty-eighth President (1913–21)

1845: Dr Thomas John Barnardo, founder of international charity which bears his name, born in Dublin.

5/7

1812: Frederick Edward Maning, naturalised Maori, born at John-ville, Co. Dublin.

Emigrated to Van Diemen's Land with father when twelve years old, adopted by Maoris as 'Pakeha Maori', meaning naturalised stranger. In due course, acquired a stretch of land, married Maori girl and adopted customs of his tribe.

In later life, under British administration, became judge in courts established to settle land titles. In that respect, regarded as important go-between by British officials and Maoris.

1828: Daniel O'Connell won Clare election, forcing government to concede Catholic Emancipation the following April.

1977: Twenty-first Dáil Éireann assembled.

Fianna Fáil returned to office with Jack Lynch as Taoiseach.

6/7

1815: Charles Bianconi, pioneer of Irish road-car service, opened first route, between Clonmel and Cahir, Co. Tipperary, a distance of 10 miles, at fare of 2d per mile.

1907: Irish Crown Jewels, valued then at £50,000, discovered to be missing from Dublin Castle.

Jewels were presented by King William IV to Order of the Knights of Saint Patrick to be worn on formal occasions by Lord Lieutenant as Grand Master of the Order. Their where-abouts remains a mystery.

7/7

1739: Death of Christian Davies, female soldier.

Enlisted in British army as a man under name of Christopher Welsh after husband press-ganged into army in Flanders. She subsequently fought at Nijmegen, Blenheim and other battles and, after separation of 13 years, found her husband. For a time the pair posed as brothers until she fractured her skull at Battle of Ramillies (1706) and had true sex discovered by army surgeons. After husband's death at Malplaquet (1709), went to London where she was awarded a pension of a shilling a day for life by Queen Anne. Returned to her native Dublin and married a soldier called Davies. Died after 25 years of obscurity and illness.

1816: Death in poverty of Richard Brinsley Sheridan, playwright and orator.

1823: John Kells Ingram, scholar and poet, born at Temple Carne, Co. Donegal. Work includes 'Who fears to speak of '98?' which appeared anonymously in *The Nation* under title, 'The Memory of the Dead' (1843).

1863: Death of William Mulready, Ennis, Co. Clare-born painter.

1922: Death from gunshot wounds received two days earlier when shot by Free State forces in O'Connell Street, Dublin, of Cathal Brugha, revolutionary,

1973: Death of General Seán MacEoin, soldier and politician known as 'The Blacksmith of Ballinalee'.

1992: Death of Pat Taaffe, jockey renowned for partnership with Arkle, greatest steeplechaser of all time.

8/7

1803: Death of Frederick Augustus Hervey, fourth Earl of Bristol and Bishop of Derry from 1768.

Hervey, in words of Earl of Charlemont, was 'a bad father, a worse husband, a determined deist, very blasphemous in his conversation and greatly addicted to intrigue and gallantry'.

1819: Sir Francis Leopold McClintock, admiral and explorer, born in Dundalk, Co. Louth.

9/7

1797: Death of Edmund Burke, orator and political philosopher. Works include *A Vindication of Natural Society* (1756) and *Reflections on the Revolution in France* (1790).

1809: John O'Donovan, scholar, noted as editor and translator of *The Annals of the Four Masters* (1848–57), born at Attateemore, Co. Kilkenny.

10/7

1927: Assassination of Kevin O'Higgins, 35-year-old Vice President of Executive Council and Minister for Justice.

Shot dead by three Republican supporters who chanced to spot him making his way to Mass, unguarded, at Booterstown, Co. Dublin.

> One of his assassins later recorded:
> When we got over to him he was not dead. This was against all the odds. It was multiple. We'd all shot him ... He held his hand up towards us clutching his rosary beads in it. He addressed us. He knew who we were. He knew why we had done it – because of the executions [O'Higgins was party to execution of seventy-seven Republicans in 1922–3.] He understood our hatred and our emotions. He then said – 'There's been too much killing in our country. The killing has got to stop. You're wrong but I forgive you. I forgive you.' We then left him and got into the car.

11/7

1793: In a pitched battle between peasant agitators and military at Taghmon, Co. Wexford, over eighty civilians were killed.

1803: Death of Thomas Hussey, Bishop and first President of St Patrick's College, Maynooth (1795–7).

1921: War of Independence ended.

Otherwise known as 'Anglo-Irish War' and 'Black and Tan War', War of Independence lasted 30 months. On British side, military effort deployed in conflict was formidable. Combined forces of police and troops, Black and Tans (deployed March 1920) and Auxiliaries (deployed August 1920) came close on forty thousand. Full strength of IRA may have been as much as fifteen thousand with no more than five thousand on active service at any one time.

Casualties among IRA and civilians during conflict estimated at seven hundred and fifty-two killed and eight hundred and sixty-six wounded. Twenty-four officially executed by British authorities. First was 18-year-old Kevin Barry. Last, just five weeks before truce, were Edward Foley and Patrick Maher from Galbally, Co. Limerick.

12/7
Orange Day

1691: Battle of Aughrim.
　　At hill of Aughrim, near Ballinasloe, Co. Galway, a twenty-thousand-strong Williamite army under command of Dutchman, General Ginkel, defeated similarly-sized Irish force under command of Frenchman, St Ruth. Aughrim was last battle in Williamite War and last major battle fought in Ireland between professional armies.

1796: First Orange Order 'Twelfth' demonstration was held.

1857: Address by Rev. Thomas Drew to members of Orange Order sparked off 10 days of continuous rioting in Belfast.

1920: Sir Edward Carson, speaking at Orange rally at Finaghy warned those assembled that they were in danger of being taken over by Sinn Féin.
　　Carson's speech marked beginning of 2 years of civil disturbances in Belfast during which nearly five hundred were killed and ten thousand driven from their jobs and homes.

1935: A revolver shot, allegedly fired at Orange procession in East Belfast or probably fired by Orangeman as provocation, started 2 months of violence in city.

1949: Death of Douglas Hyde, writer under pen-name 'An Chraoibhín Aoibhinn', scholar, translator and first President of Ireland (1938–45).

1989: Twenty-sixth Dáil Éireann assembled.
　　Fianna Fáil entered into its first coalition government, with Progressive Democrats. Charles J. Haughey elected Taoiseach.

13/7
1792: Belfast Harp Festival, held over 3 days in Assembly Room –

now Linenhall Library – concluded.

Organised by Dr James MacDonnell and other prominent residents of Belfast, concerned by decline in Irish harp music, festival attracted ten Irish harpers, most of them blind, and a Welshman named Williams. First prize awarded to Charles Fanning of Co. Cavan.

Present to record airs played by harpers was 19-year-old Edward Bunting, himself something of a musical prodigy. So enthralled was Bunting by experience that he decided to devote his future to study and collection of Irish music.

14/7

1789: Storming of the Bastille.

Though some foreigners did join in attack, unlikely that there were any Irish amongst them. Only Irishman present for certain that day was one James Francis Xavier Whyte, a Dubliner and one of fortress' seven prisoners. Born in 1730, Whyte had been captain in an Irish regiment of French army but had developed insanity and was imprisoned in 1781 at request of his family. When liberated, he was carried aloft through streets of Paris as a victim of tyranny. However, as soon as he began talking he was promptly packed off to a lunatic asylum.

1969: In Northern Ireland, first fatality of present 'troubles'.

Francis McCluskey, a 70-year-old farmer, died in mêlée between opposing factions outside Orange Hall in Dungiven, Co. Derry. To date over three thousand people have died in the Northern 'troubles'.

15/7

1802: Death in destitution in a hovel in Sydenham, Kent of 27-year-old Thomas Dermody, poet.

1865: Death of Dr James Barry, chief medical officer in British army.

In 1840s, performed first successful Caesarean section operation in medical history. Better remembered, however, for fact that 'he' was a female, daughter of Cork painter James Barry. True sex only discovered after her death. Ironically, in that same year, 1865, Elizabeth Garrett Anderson was declared to be 'first' woman doctor in Great Britain.

: Alfred Harmsworth, Lord Northcliffe, journalist, born at Chapelizod, Co. Dublin.

Northcliffe founded *Daily Mail* (1896), *Daily Mirror* (1903) and became proprietor of *The Times* in 1908.

1899: Seán Lemass, founder member of Fianna Fáil, cabinet minister in every Fianna Fáil government from 1932 and Taoiseach (1959–66), born at Ballybrack, Co. Dublin.

1907: Séamus Murphy, sculptor and stone-carver, born at Greenhill, Mallow, Co. Cork.

1927: Death, aged 59, of Countess Markievicz, revolutionary.

16/7

1850: Death of Mrs Julia Glover, leading comic actress.

1865: James Owen Hannay, clergyman and prolific writer under own name and pen-name, George A. Bermingham, born in Belfast. Many works include *The Spirit and Origin of Christian Monasticism* (1925) and *Mrs Miller's Aunt* (1936).

17/7

1798: 30-year-old Henry Joy McCracken, United Irishman, hanged in Belfast.

> The time allowed him had now expired; about 5 p.m. he was ordered to the place of execution – the old market-house – the ground of which had been given to the town by his great grandfather. I took his arm and together we walked to the fatal spot.
> … Harry begged I would go. Clasping my arms around him (I did not weep till then) I said I could bear anything but leaving him. Three times he kissed me and entreated I would go, and fearing any further refusal would disturb the last moments of my dearest brother, I suffered myself to be led away.
> … I was told afterwards that poor Harry stood when I left him and watched me till I was out of sight; that he then attempted to speak to the people, but that the noise of the

trampling of the horses was so great that it was impossible he could be heard; that he then resigned himself to his fate, and the multitude who were present at that moment uttered cries which seemed more like one loud and long continued shriek than the expression of grief or terror on similar occasions....

– Mary Anne McCracken

1871: John Andrews, second Prime Minister of Northern Ireland (1940–43), born at Comber, Co. Down.

1935: Death of George William Russell, poet, theosophist, agricultural economist, editor and essayist, better known by pseudonym, Æ. Works include *The Hero in Man* (1909).

18/7

1794: Feargus O'Connor, Chartist leader, born in Connorville, Co. Cork.

1874: Cathal Brugha, revolutionary, born in Dublin.

1938: Douglas 'Wrongway' Corrigan landed at Baldonnel aerodrome, Dublin.
   The 31-year-old from Los Angeles crossed Atlantic from New York in battered 9-year-old curtiss Robin single-engined aircraft. With no luggage and $15 in his pocket, he told reporters that he believed he was 'on his way home'.

19/7

1735: Garrett Wellesley or Wesley, first Earl of Mornington and father of Duke of Wellington, born in Dublin.
   Son of Richard Colley who changed name to allow him inherit cousin's estate, bequeathed to him on that condition. Five sons all became famous; one duke, one marquis, two barons and one prebendary of Durham.

1920: Sectarian violence erupted in Derry city.
   Nineteen died and over fifty wounded in 4 days of continuous violence.

20/7

1616: Death in Rome of Hugh O'Neill, Earl of Tyrone.

After almost 9 years in exile, Ulster chieftain, in words of Seán O'Faolain, had become 'habituated to melancholy and homelessness and the routine of idle days'. O'Neill buried with great pomp beside his son in Church of San Pietra di Montario.

1982: In London, eleven British soldiers, including seven bandsmen killed by Provisional IRA bombs.

21/7

1928: John B. Keane, playwright and novelist, born in Listowel, Co. Kerry. Work includes plays *Sive* (1959) and *The Field* (1965) and novel *Durango* (1992).

1972: 'Bloody Friday' in Belfast.

In spate of bombings, most intense burst of violence hitherto carried out by Provisional IRA, nine people killed and over a hundred injured.

1976: Assassination of British ambassador to Ireland, Christopher Ewart-Biggs.

Ambassador and a senior British civil servant in Northern Ireland office killed when 200-pound Provisional IRA mine blew up their car near ambassador's official residence in Sandyford, Co. Dublin.

22/7

1817: William Sadler made first balloon crossing of Irish Sea, from Dublin to Anglesey, Wales, in 6 hours.

1902: Death of Dr Thomas William Croke, Archbishop of Cashel and Emly, staunch supporter of Land League and one of first patrons of GAA.

1985: 'Moving Statue' at Ballinspittle, Co. Cork.

Two ladies taking an evening stroll claimed that a statue of Virgin Mary, sited at grotto on outskirts of village, had moved. Village subsequently became place of pilgrimage, attracting as many as 10,000 visitors daily.

23/7

1693: Death of Patrick Sarsfield, Earl of Lucan.

Died of fever aggravated by injuries sustained 4 days previously when fighting under flag of France at Battle of Landen. 'Would to God this was shed for Ireland', he reputedly remarked on seeing blood from his wounds.

1803: Robert Emmet's 'rising' in Thomas Street, Dublin.

At about 9 p.m. Emmet led about one hundred undisciplined followers to attack Dublin Castle. En route, Lord Chief Justice, Lord Kilwarden, and his nephew, Rev. Richard Wolfe, dragged from their coach and murdered. Emmet subsequently fled to Dublin mountains and was arrested a month later.

24/7

1750: John Philpot Curran, lawyer, born at Newmarket, Co. Cork.

Strong advocate of Catholic emancipation and severe critic of government patronage and corruption. Before and after rebellion of 1798, defended a number of United Irishmen, including Wolfe Tone. Refused, however, to represent Robert Emmet. When he discovered that his daughter, Sarah, was secretly engaged to him, had her banished from his home.

Renowned as brilliant orator and wit, most famous saying was a serious one. In a legal case, in 1790, over election of Dublin's Lord Mayor, he warned:

> The condition upon which God hath given liberty to man is eternal vigilance; which condition if he break, servitude is at once the consequence of his crime and the punishment of his guilt.

1990: In Northern Ireland, three policemen and a nun killed by Provisional IRA bomb near Armagh city.

25/7

1917: Irish Convention, to discuss 'how to effect a reconciliation of the aspirations of Ulster with those of the rest of Ireland' held opening session.

Chaired by southern Unionist, Sir Horace Plunkett, and attended by nominees of British government, Protestant and Catholic Churches, trades unions, industry and various political parties, with exception of Sinn Féin who abstained, con-

vention finally reported in April 1918. In report, overwhelming
majority of nominees agreed on form of Home Rule for Ireland
which incorporated concessions to Unionists more generous
than any that British parliament included in any of their Home
Rule Bills. Despite such generosity from Nationalist side, Ulster
Unionists would not agree. In June 1917, even before convention met, British Prime Minister, Lloyd George, had privately
promised Unionist leader, Edward Carson, that nothing would
be done about convention's conclusions and recommendations
if Ulster Unionists did not agree. Convention proved impos-
sibility of seeking settlement on basis of united, self-governing
Ireland.

1919: Death of Sir Samuel McCaughey, the 'Sheep King'.
      Born near Ballymena, Co. Antrim in 1835, owned a number
of highly profitable sheep stations in Victoria and New South
Wales. At one stage, was shearing one million sheep a year.
Died unmarried, having bequeathed nearly £2 million for education and charitable purposes.

26/7

1782: John Field, composer and pianist, renowned for his noc-
      turnes, born in Dublin, son of a theatre violinist.

1856: George Bernard Shaw, playwright and Nobel Prize for Lit-
      erature winner (1925), born in Dublin, only son of un-
      successful wholesale merchant. Works include *John Bull's
      Other Island* (1904), *The Doctor's Dilemma* (1906) and *War
      Issues for Irishmen* (1918).

1914: The *Asgard* landed at Howth with over 1,000 German rifles
      and 29,000 rounds of ammunition for Irish Volunteers.
      Later that day, troops opened fire on crowd at Bachelor's
Walk, Dublin, killing four and wounding thirty-seven.

1918: Death, aged 31, of Major Edward 'Mick' Mannock VC.
      Born in Ballincollig, near Cork City, was most celebrated
fighter pilot of First World War, shooting down over 70 enemy
planes in 14 months. Died after being hit by enemy ground fire
while flying behind German lines in France.

1987: In sport, Stephen Roche became first Irishman to win cycling's premier event, the Tour de France.

27/7

1669: Molly Malone, celebrated fishmonger and subject of a ballad which became Dublin's anthem, christened at St Werburgh's Church.

1805: Death of Brian Merriman, poet.

'Died on Saturday morning in Old Clare Street after a few hours illness, Mr Bryan Merryman, teacher of mathematics...'

Obituary notice in *General Advertiser and Limerick Gazette* on death of Brian Mac Giolla Meidhre, Brian Merriman, did not mention that he had composed perhaps the greatest humorous poem in Irish language: *Cúirt An Mheán Oíche – The Midnight Court*. Neither did it mention, as some critics suggest, that Irish literature in Irish language may be said to have died with him.

Born at Ennistymon, Co. Clare probably attended hedge school. In 1770, was teaching in village of Feakle and, after marrying in middle age, settled in Limerick City where he continued to teach until his death.

1830: John O'Leary, Fenian, born in Tipperary town.

1866: First submarine cable link, between Valentia Island, Co. Kerry and Trinity Bay, Newfoundland, was completed.

28/7

1689: Siege of Derry ended.

Throughout April and May, after dismissal of governor, Robert Lundy, seven thousand Derry defenders had resisted attempts by Jacobites to break through. In June, crowded city came under increased shelling; in one 5-day period 159 bombs landed within walls. Casualties among over twenty thousand citizens soared and defenders lost up to a thousand men. With boom composed of tree trunks fastened with cables blocking access to the port, inhabitants fought starvation on diet of cats, dogs and rats. In late July, a boy succeeded in delivering news of plight to Major General Kirk who had remained with his fleet outside the boom. 105-day siege resulted in victory for defenders at cost of ten thousand lives.

1895: John Charles McQuaid, Archbishop of Dublin (1940–72), born at Cootehill, Co. Cavan.

1943: Cloghane, Co. Kerry air disaster.
Ten died when civilian plane carrying mainly RAF passengers en route from Lisbon to Foynes airport crashed on slopes of Mount Brandon.

29/7

1848: 'The Ballingarry Fracas'.
Otherwise known as 'Battle of the Widow McCormack's cabbage garden': Young Ireland leader, William Smith O'Brien, and a few dozen ill-armed followers laid siege on about forty policemen who had barricaded themselves in Widow McCormack's home at Ballingarry, Co. Tipperary. No police were killed or injured but they shot dead two of besiegers and wounded several others. Siege was lifted after a few hours when police reinforcements arrived. Smith O'Brien arrested a week later at Thurles railway station.

1883: James Carey, informer, was assassinated.
Dublin councillor who, by turning King's evidence against accomplices in Phoenix Park Murders of May 1881, had sent five to gallows. Shot dead aboard steamship *Melrose* en route from Port Elizabeth to Natal, heading for new life along with wife and seven children. Assassin was Patrick O'Donnell from Gweedore, Co. Donegal, who maintained that he 'was never commissioned by any body of men, directly or indirectly, to pursue the informer', and was hanged on 17 December 1883.

30/7

1928: At ninth Olympic Games in Amsterdam, Dr Pat O'Callaghan, from Kanturk, Co. Cork, won gold medal in hammer event.
Weighing 17 stone, aged 22 and described by Reuter's reporter as a 'great boyish figure of a man, with a mass of golden hair', O'Callaghan took gold with a throw of 168 feet, 7.5 inches. Though several Irishmen had won Olympic gold before,

all had done so under flags of other countries. O'Callaghan's victory was Ireland's first as an independent nation.

1972: In Northern Ireland, 'Operation Motorman', the breaking down of barricades by British troops in Catholic and Protestant 'no-go' areas of Belfast and Derry, took place.

1990: Ian Gow, Conservative MP was killed by a Provisional IRA bomb as he left his home in Sussex.

31/7

1893: The Gaelic League (Conradh Na Gaeilge), to preserve and promote the Irish language, established by Douglas Hyde, Eoin MacNeill and Fr Eugene O'Growney.

1917: Death, in action at Ypres, of 26-year-old Francis Ledwidge, poet. Almost entire work in two volumes: *Songs of the Fields* (1916) and *Songs of the Peace* (1917)

1972: Nine people died, including a 9-year-old girl, when Provisional IRA bombs exploded without warning in village of Claudy, Co. Derry.

August

1/8

1915: Funeral to Glasnevin Cemetery, Dublin, of Jeremiah O'Donovan Rossa.

Patrick Pearse, dressed in uniform of Irish Volunteers, delivered funeral oration, ending in famous words:

... the fools, the fools, the fools! – they have left us our Fenian dead, and while Ireland holds these graves, Ireland unfree shall never be at peace.

1931: Seán Ó Riada, composer and musician, born in Cork.

1986: Sudden death in Lourdes of Monsignor James Horan, parish priest of Knock, Co. Mayo and founder of Knock airport, latterly Connaught Regional Airport.

2/8

1649: Battle of Rathmines, in which Royalist forces under Duke of Ormond were defeated by parliamentary leader, Colonel Michael Jones.

1812: Death of Edward Smyth, sculptor.

Born in Co. Meath, is best known for statue of Charles Lucas in Dublin City Hall and ornamental work on Custom House and Irish House of Lords.

1849: Arrival in Ireland on a state visit of Queen Victoria.

The 30-year-old Victoria, accompanied by Prince Albert and her four children, visited Cork, Dublin and Belfast. Subsequent visits, in 1853, 1861 and 1900. Last visit, during which she issued orders for a new regiment – the Irish Guards – was recorded on film, the oldest known taken in Ireland.

3/8

1823: Thomas Francis Meagher, Young Irelander, known as 'Meagher of the Sword', born in Waterford.

1916: Sir Roger Casement, patriot, hanged at Pentonville prison for treason.
     Born in Dublin and reared in Glens of Antrim, spent 20 years in British colonial service during which time he won an international reputation for humanitarian activities. Knighted in 1911 for his public services

4/8

1799: Death of James Caulfield, Earl of Charlemont and leader of Irish Volunteers.

1805: Sir William Rowan Hamilton, mathematician and astronomer, born in Dublin.

1914: Britain declared war on Germany.

1927: Death of John Dillon, Nationalist MP who led the anti-Parnellite faction after split in Irish Party in 1891.

5/8

1888: Death of Philip Henry Sheridan, United States general.

1956: Death of John Andrews second Prime Minister of Northern Ireland (1940–43).

6/8

1775: Daniel O'Connell, 'The Liberator' born at Carhen, Cahirciveen, Co. Kerry.
     Adopted as a child by prosperous uncle, Maurice 'Hunting Cap' O'Connell, head of old Catholic family of O'Connells, and

reared by him at Derrynane.

Universally acknowledged 'king' of Ireland in his hey-day, great achievement was Catholic Emancipation (1829), overshadowed by failure to win repeal of Act of Union.

7/8

1942: Death of Michael O'Flanagan, priest and Republican, who said prayers at First Dáil, in January 1919.

1943: Death of Sarah Purser, artist, portrait painter and founder, in 1903, of acclaimed stained-glass workshop 'An Túr Gloine' (The Tower of Glass).

8/8

1647: Battle of Dungan's Hill, near Trim, Co. Meath, in which General Thomas Preston, leader of Old English Catholic forces was heavily defeated by parliamentary commander, Michael Jones.

1958: Death of Brendan Bracken, newspaper publisher and private secretary to Winston Churchill from outbreak of Second World War.

1984: Death of Denis Johnston, actor and dramatist. Works include *The Moon on the Yellow River* (1931) and *In Search of Swift* (1959).

1992: Michael Carruth from Dublin won Ireland's first boxing gold medal, in welterweight division, at Olympic Games in Barcelona.

9/8

1886: Death of Sir Samuel Ferguson, poet, antiquary and one of most influential participants in Irish literary revival of 1830s. Most important antiquarian work is *Ogham Inscriptions in Ireland, Scotland & Wales* (1887), published posthumously.

1971: Internment introduced in Northern Ireland.

In early hours of morning, over three hundred men arrested and taken to detention centres. By May 1972 there were twelve hundred people detained or interned without trial. Internment ended in December 1975.

10/8

1900: Death of Charles Russell, Baron Russell of Killowen, lawyer.

Climax of his brilliant legal career came during Parnell Commission of 1888–90, when, representing Parnell against *The Times*, he tore to shreds the evidence of the forger, Richard Pigott. In 1894, was appointed Lord Chief Justice, first Catholic to be appointed to the position since Reformation.

1975: Death of Robert Childers Barton, Nationalist and last surviving signatory of Anglo–Irish Treaty of 1921.

1976: In Belfast, three children killed and their mother badly injured when struck by car driven by Provisional IRA member who was being chased by British army patrol.

Deaths of Maguire children led to founding of widely supported though short-lived 'Women's Peace Movement', later the 'Peace People', led by Betty Williams, Máiréad Corrigan and Ciarán McKeown.

11/8

1835: Rev. Henry Grattan Guinness, evangelist and one of greatest religious orators of nineteenth century, born in Dún Laoghaire.

1974: Death of Liam Ó Briain, patriot and scholar.

12/8
Apprentice Boys' Day

1796: Kilmainham Gaol, Dublin, received its first inmates.

Kilmainham was constructed during 1780s as debtors' prison for Co. Dublin. First of generations of political prisoners to be lodged there was United Irishman, Henry Joy McCracken who was incarcerated on 6 October 1796. Last prisoners were released from Kilmainham during summer of 1924.

1822: Death by suicide of Robert Stewart, Lord Castlereagh, architect of Act of Union (1800).

1914: Death at Newark, New Jersey of John Philip Holland, inventor of modern submarine.

1922: Death of Arthur Griffith, political leader and founder of Sinn Féin (1905).

1969: Derry riots.
Disturbances following traditional Apprentice Boys' March led to two days and nights of rioting. Peace eventually restored when British troops arrived in city at 5.00 p.m. on 14 August. Derry disturbances were followed by more serious, sectarian violence in Belfast.

1984: John Treacy of Ireland won a silver medal in the marathon at twenty-third Olympic Games in Los Angeles.

13/8

1971: Death of Sir Shane Leslie, writer. Works include *The End of a Chapter* (1916), *Verses in Peace and War* (1922) and *Letters of Mrs FitzHerbert* (1940).

1974: Death of Kate O'Brien, novelist and dramatist. Works include *Distinguished Villa* (1926), *Without My Cloak* (1931) and *Teresa of Avila* (1951).

14/8

1598: Battle of the Yellow Ford (Co. Tyrone) – Gaelic Ireland's greatest victory.
Irish forces under Hugh O'Neill, Earl of Tyrone, heavily defeated Crown forces under Sir Henry Bagenal, who was killed in action. A contemporary wrote: 'Since the time the English set foot in Ireland they never received a greater overthrow, 13

stout captains being slain and over 1,500 column soldiers'.

1983: Eamonn Coughlan won 5,000 metres title at World Athletics Championships in Helsinki, a success comparable to the 1,500 metres triumph by fellow countryman Ronnie Delaney in Melbourne Olympics 27 years previously.

15/8

1649: Oliver Cromwell, 'Lord Lieutenant and General for the Parliament of England' landed in Dublin at head of 10,000-strong army.

According to a contemporary account 'he was received with all possible demonstrations of joy; the great guns echoing forth their welcome and the acclamation of the people resounding in every street.' A week later he issued a proclamation forbidding 'profaning, swearing, drinking, cursing, which were said to be the daily practice'.

1843: Daniel O'Connell addressed his biggest 'monster meeting' at Tara, Co. Meath.

During the proceedings, attended by 750,000 people – the largest gathering held in Ireland until the Eucharistic Congress of 1932 – O'Connell was crowned 'King of Ireland' by sculptor John Hogan and author John O'Callaghan.

1880: Derrybeg, Co. Donegal flooding tragedy.

As Canon James McFadden was celebrating Mass of the Assumption, violent thunderstorm led to flooding within chapel. Though he succeeded in finishing the Mass, five members of congregation were drowned.

1917: Jack Lynch, renowned hurler and footballer, leader of Fianna Fáil (1966–79) and Taoiseach (1966–73, 1977–9), born in Cork.

16/8

1911: Death in Sydney of Patrick Francis Moran, Australia's first cardinal.

Nephew of Cardinal Paul Cullen, Archbishop of Dublin, was ordained to priesthood by special permission, at age of 22.

1884, went to Australia as Archbishop of Sydney and a year later became Australia's first cardinal. Staunch supporter of Australian federation and of Irish Home Rule movement.

17/8

1878: Oliver St John Gogarty, surgeon, wit, writer and model for Buck Mulligan in James Joyce's *Ulysses*, born in Dublin.

18/8

1728: James Caulfield, Earl of Charlemont, commander-in-chief of Irish Volunteers and patron of the arts, born in Dublin.

1882: Maamtrasna murders, Co. Galway.

Hired by a local gombeen man, a number of assassins set out to murder alleged sheep-stealer in Maamtrasna Valley on Mayo–Galway border. In the process they also murdered his wife, mother, daughter and son.

Under pressure to find scapegoats for Irish crime, authorities connived to withhold evidence and manipulate witnesses so as to secure convictions of eight men. Three were sentenced to death, the remainder to penal servitude for life.

On eve of execution, in written depositions before a magistrate, two of the condemned men admitted own guilt while affirming innocence of third, Myles Joyce. Lord Lieutenant, Earl Spencer, refused to grant reprieve or inquiry.

Subsequently, a Crown witness retracted his evidence and declared that Joyce and four of those imprisoned were innocent. Nevertheless, surviving prisoners not released until 1902.

1973: Death of Sir Basil Brooke, Viscount Brookeborough, Prime Minister of Northern Ireland (1943–63).

As Minister of Agriculture, from 1933, delivered series of speeches urging Protestants not to employ Catholics because they were disloyal and 'out to destroy us as a body'. He himself dismissed a hundred and twenty-five Catholic workers on his Fermanagh estates. Speeches set tone for discriminatory policy on employment in Northern Ireland which became one of principal grievances leading to political upheavals of late 1960s. In his 20 years as Prime Minister, had no official contact with trades unions or Catholics.

19/8

1504: Battle of Knockdoe (Co. Galway), in which Lord Deputy, Great Earl of Kildare – using firearms for first time in an Irish battle – defeated southern chieftains, led by his son-in-law, Ulick Burke of Clanrickard.

1887: Francis Ledwidge, poet, born at Slane, Co. Meath. Works include *Songs of the Fields* (1916) and *Songs of Peace* (1917).

20/8

1778: Bernardo O'Higgins, father of Chilean independence, born in Chile.

His father, Ambrose O'Higgins came from Co. Meath. Bernardo played leading role in Chilean independence movement. After proclamation in 1818 of Chile's independence from Spain, became Supreme Director and ruled country as virtual dictator until 1823.

1798: Dr Richard Madden, historian, born in Dublin. Publications include *Breathings of Prayer in Many Lands* (1838) and *The United Irishmen: Their Lives and Times* (4 vols, 1842–6).

1988: In Northern Ireland, eight British soldiers killed and twenty-seven injured when Provisional IRA bomb blew up their bus between Ballygawley and Omagh, Co. Tyrone.

21/8

1879: Apparitions at Knock, Co. Mayo.

At 8 p.m. approximately, three life-sized figures seen, surrounded by light, at western gable of local chapel. One in middle immediately identified as Our Lady, eyes lifted to heaven and hands raised to shoulders with palms inwards. To her right was St Joseph, head bowed respectfully towards her and on her left a figure identified by one of witnesses as St John the Evangelist. To the left of St John was an altar on which stood a cross and a lamb and around which some saw angels' wings.

Vision lasted for about 2 hours from broad daylight to darkness and was seen by at least twenty-two people. Though it was raining and all witnesses were thoroughly drenched, no rain fell on figures or on wall behind them.

1882: Death of Charles J. Kickham, Fenian and novelist, Works include *Knocknagow, or, The Homes of Tipperary* (1879).

1970: In Northern Ireland, Social Democratic and Labour Party (SDLP) was formed with Gerry Fitt as leader.

22/8

1802: Death of George Thomas, the 'Rajah from Tipperary'.

Born near Roscrea, served as mercenary soldier under various Indian rulers and in 1797 made himself Rajah of State of Hariana, a wide territory which he extended through frequent raids on neighbours. As ruler, founded mint and gun factories and proposed to British government that he should invade Punjab on their behalf. 1802, deposed in Sikh uprising and escorted to British frontier. Intended to return to Ireland but died from fever at Bahrampur, Bengal.

1922: Death, aged 32, of General Michael Collins.

Commander-in-chief of government forces, died from single bullet wound in head received when his convoy was ambushed by Republicans at Béal na Bláth, between Macroom and Bandon, Co. Cork.

1972: In Northern Ireland, nine died when Provisional IRA bomb exploded prematurely at Newry Custom House, Co. Down.

23/8

1170: Richard FitzGilbert de Clare, Earl of Pembroke, popularly known as 'Strongbow' and one of Ireland's most renowned invaders, landed at Passage, Co. Waterford with a thousand men-at-arms.

1826: Death in Sydney of Michael Dwyer, insurgent leader.

Born in Glen of Imaal, Co. Wicklow, took part in Rising of 1798 and for 5 years afterwards defied all efforts by Crown forces to capture him. 1803, surrendered voluntarily and was transported to New South Wales. 1815, became High Constable of Sydney.

24/8

1803: Death of James Napper Tandy, United Irishman immortalised in ballad 'The Wearing of the Green'.

1896: Liam O'Flaherty, writer, born on Inishmore, Aran Islands. Works include *The Informer* (1925) and *Famine* (1937).

1962: Death of Anew McMaster, last of touring actor-managers who brought Shakespeare to rural Ireland.

1968: Northern Ireland Civil Rights Association (NICRA) first march; a six-mile 'freedom march' from Coalisland to Dungannon, Co. Tyrone.

1990: Brian Keenan, a teacher from Belfast, released after spending 52 months as a hostage in Beirut.

25/8

1580: Battle of Glenmalure, Co. Wicklow, in which Fiach Mac-Hugh O'Byrne totally defeated forces of Deputy, Lord Grey de Wilton.

1764: Jemmy Hope, 'The Weaver of Templepatrick', United Irishman, born in Templepatrick, Co. Antrim.

1863: Fr Eugene O'Growney, leading Irish language revivalist and first vice-president of Gaelic League, born at Ballyfallon, Co. Meath.

1882: Seán T. Ó Ceallaigh, founder-member of Sinn Féin and second President of Ireland (1945–59), born in Dublin.

26/8

1913: Great Dublin 'Lock-out' began with strike by city's tram-workers, members of James Larkin's Irish Transport and General Workers' Union (ITGWU).
    Though tram-workers' strike only partially successful, subsequent strike action by dockers led to all ITGWU members being locked out by William Martin Murphy-led Employers' Federation. By end of September, estimated hundred thousand

Dubliners faced starvation.

As lock-out continued, food supplies from British trade unions were shipped to Dublin and soup kitchens in Liberty Hall provided basic food for thousands of destitute. However, by turn of year, supplies had dwindled to a trickle and in January and February 1914, men gradually returned to work.

Outcome a drawn battle since employers failed to break Larkin's Union.

27/8

1870: *Oceanic,* first modern liner, built by Harland and Wolff, Belfast for White Star Line, was launched.

1874: Death of John Henry Foley, sculptor.

Regarded in his day as leading sculptor in these islands. Works include statues of Edmund Burke and Oliver Goldsmith outside gates of Trinity College, Dublin, and statue of Henry Grattan, in College Green. At time of his death, was working on O'Connell monument in Sackville St, now O'Connell St, Dublin.

1979: Mountbatten murder.

Shortly after 11.30 a.m. Lord Louis Mountbatten, his nephew and a 15-year-old local schoolboy were killed when Provisional IRA bomb exploded on board their boat *Shadow V* off Mullaghmore, Co. Sligo.

: Warrenpoint massacre, Northern Ireland.

That afternoon, in double explosion and gun attack, Provisional IRA killed eighteen British soldiers at Narrow Water, near Warrenpoint, Co. Down.

1992 Official RUC death-toll for 20 years of Northern Ireland disturbances reached three thousand when 20-year-old Hugh McKibbin was shot dead in West Belfast.

28/8

1814: Joseph Sheridan Le Fanu, journalist and novelist, born in Dublin. Works include *The House by the Churchyard* (1863) and *Uncle Silas* (1864).

1815: Mary Martin, novelist known as 'The Princess of Conne-mara' born at Ballynahinch Castle, Co. Galway. Works include *St Etienne* (1845) and *Julia Howard* (1850).

29/8

1803: Death at Poughkeepsie, New York State, of Samuel Neilson, United Irishman and founder of *Northern Star*, organ of United Irishmen in north of Ireland.

1844: Death of Edmund Ignatius Rice, founder of Irish Christian Brothers (1820).

1871: Jack Butler Yeats, artist and writer, son of painter John Butler Yeats and younger brother of poet W.B. Yeats, born in London.

1975: Death of Eamon De Valera, revolutionary, politician and third President of Ireland (1959–73).

30/8

1855: Death of Feargus O'Connor, Chartist leader.
Barrister and nephew of United Irishman, Arthur O'Connor, was leader of Chartist movement in Britain during its hey-day in late 1830s and early 1840s. 1847, elected MP for Nottingham.

31/8

1602: Sudden death at Simancas in Spain of Red Hugh O'Don-nell, chief of O'Donnells of Donegal and ally of Hugh O'Neill in Nine Years War.
Aged about 30 at the time, was poisoned by James Blake of Galway, probably with cognisance of Sir George Carew, President of Munster.

1767: Henry Joy McCracken, United Irishman, born in Belfast.

1806: Charles Lever, novelist, born in Dublin. Works include *Harry Lorrequer* (1840) and *Charles O'Malley* (1841).

September

1/9

1737: First edition of *Belfast News Letter*.

 News Letter is oldest daily newspaper in Ireland and second only to *Lloyd's List* (1719) as oldest newspaper in these islands. Founded by Francis Joy (1697–1790), grandfather of United Irishman, Henry Joy McCracken.

1830: 'The Wild Colonial Boy', Australian bushranger, shot dead in gun-battle with police at Campbelltown, Sydney.

 Contrary to lyrics of popular ballad, 'The Wild Colonial Boy' was born in Dublin as John Donohue. Transported from Ireland in 1824, escaped gallows 3 years later and was thereafter continually pursued by the law.

1856: John Redmond, leader of Parnellite MPs after split in Irish Party in 1891 and leader of reunited Irish Party from 1900, born at Ballytrant, Co. Wexford.

1864: Sir Roger Casement, British colonial service official and patriot, born at Sandycove, Co. Dublin.

2/9

1865: Death of Sir William Rowan Hamilton, mathematician, linguist and astronomer.

 Born in Dublin in 1805, wrote extensively on mathematical problems. *The Elements of Quaternions*, published posthumously, ranked him with Descartes in terms of originality and insight.

3/9

1513: Death, from wounds received in skirmish with O'Mores of
Leix, of Garret More FitzGerald, the Great Earl of Kildare
and virtual ruler of Ireland for 40 years.

1842: John Devoy, Fenian, and one of most influential leaders in
Irish-American organisation, Clan Na Gael, born at Kill, Co.
Kildare.

1963: Death of Louis MacNeice, poet and broadcaster. Poetry collections include *Holes in the Sky* (1947) and *The Strings are
False* (published posthumously, 1965).

4/9

1607: 'The Flight of the Earls'.
Hugh O'Neill, Earl of Tyrone, and Ruairí O'Donnell, Earl of
Tyrconnell, along with families – ninety-nine persons in all –
sailed from Rathmullan, Co. Donegal, into exile on Continent.

1828: Annadown, Co. Galway, boating tragedy.

> Connaught ... Accident ... An old row boat, in a rotten and
> leaky condition, started from Annadown, about eight miles
> up Lough Corrib, having about thirty-one persons on board,
> who were going to the fair of Galway. When opposite
> Bushy-park, within two miles of Galway, she suddenly went
> down and all on board perished, except twelve persons,
> who were rescued by another boat. The accident occurred
> by a sheep putting its leg through one of the planks, which
> produced a leak. In order to stop it, one of the passengers
> applied his great coat to the aperture, and stamped it with
> his foot; in doing so, he started one of the planks altogether,
> and the boat immediately sank'.
>
> – *Annual Review of World Events*, 1928

1851: John Dillon, MP who became chairman of anti-Parnellite
group following split in Irish Party in 1891, born at Blackrock, Co. Dublin.

1989: Century Radio, Republic of Ireland's first licensed commercial national radio station began broadcasting in Dublin.

5/9

1820: Edmund Ignatius Rice's congregation, better known as Irish Christian Brothers, approved by Pope Pius VII as 'the Institute of the Brothers of the Christian Schools of Ireland'.

1926: Drumcollagher, Co. Limerick fire disaster.
Forty-eight died when fire broke out in local picture house during a screening of *The Ten Commandments*.

1931: First edition of the *Irish Press*.
Founded by Eamon De Valera as forum for Fianna Fáil and did much to assist that party in gaining power after general election of February 1932. First editor was Frank Gallagher.

1980: Death of Eric Cross, writer. Best remembered for *The Tailor and Ansty* (1942).

6/9

1813: Isaac Butt, barrister, politician and founder, in 1870, of Irish Home Rule Movement, born at Glenfin, Ballybofey, Co. Donegal.

1987: Cyclist Stephen Roche became first Irish rider to win World Professional Road Race Championship.

7/9

1892: In New Orleans, John L. Sullivan, 'The Boston Strong Boy' met 'Gentleman' James J. Corbett in first world heavyweight boxing contest under Queensberry rules.
Son of Irish labourer from Tralee, Co. Kerry and Irishwoman from Athlone, Co. Westmeath, Sullivan was 34 years old and out of ring for 3 years when he faced new hero of Irish America, Californian James J. Corbett. A younger man and a master boxer, Corbett took crown with a knockout in twenty-first round.

1948: At press conference in Canada, Taoiseach John A. Costello declared that Irish State was a Republic and that External Relations Act would be repealed.
Republic of Ireland was formally inaugurated on Easter Monday 1949.

8/9

1798: Battle of Ballinamuck, Co. Longford, in which General
Humbert's French-Irish forces defeated by Lord Cornwallis.
    Having surrendered to Cornwallis, Humbert's defeated
Frenchmen were repatriated; Irish followers were massacred
that same afternoon.

1933: Fine Gael Party, a merger of Cumann na nGaedheal Party,
National Guard (Blueshirts) and National Centre Party was
founded, with General Eoin O'Duffy as leader.

9/9

1649: Siege of Drogheda, by forces of Oliver Cromwell, began.
    In a general massacre, almost entire Royalist garrison of
about three thousand, along with an unspecified number of
civilians, were put to the sword. In Cromwell's words: 'A right-
eous judgment of God upon those barbarous wretches who
have imbued their hands in so much innocent blood'.

1887: At Mitchelstown, Co. Cork, police opened fire on a large
crowd being addressed by Nationalist MP John Dillon, killing three and wounding two others.

1922: Third Dáil Éireann assembled.
    W.T. Cosgrave elected head of provisional government.

10/9

1813: Fall of Ireland's largest recorded meteorite – 65-pound
'Limerick Stone'.

1831: Jeremiah O'Donovan Rossa, Fenian, born at Rosscarbery,
Co. Cork.

1914: Captain Terence O'Neill, Lord O'Neill of the Maine, Prime
Minister of Northern Ireland (1963–9), born at Ahoghill, Co.
Antrim.

11/9

1832: Death of Molesworth Phillips, lieutenant colonel and companion to Captain Cook.

Born in Swords, Co. Dublin, in 1755, sailed with Captain Cook on what proved to be his last voyage. On St Valentine's Day 1779, was among group of marines who landed with Cook on Sandwich Islands to recover a stolen boat. Attacked by natives who killed Cook, Phillips was one of just two marines who managed to escape and return to ship.

1954: Death of Robert Smyllie, distinguished journalist and editor of *The Irish Times*.

12/9

1847: Battle of Churubusco (Mexico City); execution of sixty Irishmen serving under Mexican flag.

Irishmen were members of St Patrick's Battalion, formed by Captain John Reilly and made up primarily of Irish soldiers who deserted US army to take up cause of Mexico which was at war with US. Executed on orders of General Winfield Scott. 'The heroic Irish' annually commemorated, on this date, in a ceremony in Mexico City.

1907: Louis MacNeice, poet and broadcaster, born in Belfast, son of a clergyman. Work includes *Autumn Journal* (1938–9) and *Autumn Sequel* (1954).

1912: Death of Fr Matthew Russell, writer and editor.

Born in Newry, Co. Down, was editor of *Irish Monthly* which he founded in 1873 and edited until his death. Journal provided outlet for many promising young writers including W.B. Yeats.

13/9

1803: Death of John Barry, commodore in US navy, renowned as 'Father of the American Navy'.

1845: *Gardener's Chronicle and Horticultural Gazette* reported famine in Ireland.

With 'general failures' recorded in 1740 and 1800, potato crop badly affected in various parts of country throughout 1830s. For 1845 crop, forecasts were good, *The Times* in late July reporting that 'an early and productive harvest [was] every-where expected'. Then came news from Isle of Wight and southern counties of England of outbreak of disease – same hitherto unknown disease which in previous year had devastated potato crop of North America. *Gardener's Chronicle and Horticultural Gazette* made dramatic, though not unexpected announcement – 'We stop the press with very great regret to announce that the potato murrain has unequivocally declared itself in Ireland'.

Great Famine, 1845–9, claimed an estimated one million lives. A further one-and-a-half million emigrated.

14/9

1852: Death of Arthur Wellesley, first Duke of Wellington and field marshal.

1907: Edel Mary Quinn, Legion of Mary envoy to Africa, born at Greenane, Kanturk, Co. Cork.

1971: A new Loyalist Party (later named Democratic Unionist Party) was founded by Rev. Ian Paisley and Desmond Boal.

1989: University of Limerick – first university to be established since foundation of the State – was inaugurated.

15/9

1851: Sir William Whitla, physician and first MP for Queen's University, Belfast (1918–23), born in Monaghan town.

1866: Death of John Blake Dillon, Nationalist and co-founder of *The Nation* (1842).

1974: Death of Mrs Sydney Czira, née Sydney Gifford, Republican and journalist under pen-name John Brennan.

16/9

1701: Death of King James II.

1830: Patrick Francis Moran, who, in 1885 became Australia's first cardinal, born at Leighlinbridge, Co. Carlow.

1840: Death, aged 30, of Thomas Davis, poet, Nationalist and co-founder of *The Nation* newspaper.

1925: Charles J. Haughey, leader of Fianna Fáil (1979–92) and three times Taoiseach, born in Castlebar, Co. Mayo.

1941: Sixteen Irish soldiers killed by explosion while conducting tests with anti-tank mines in Glen of Imaal, Co. Wicklow – worst disaster in annuals of Irish defence forces.

1945: Death of John McCormack, operatic and concert tenor.

17/9

1862: Battle of Antietam Creek (American Civil War).

At Bloody Lane, where heaviest fighting in bloodiest one-day battle of civil war took place, Thomas Francis Meagher's Irish Brigade fixed bayonets and charged, green flags flying at head of its three regiments – 69th, 88th and 63rd – as they stormed what was a natural rifle pit, and a North Carolina Regiment poured 'devastating' fire into them at close range. A Confederate brigadier-general remarked that 'for five minutes they bravely stood telling fire at about 80 yards, which my whole brigade delivered. They then fell back a short distance, rallied, were driven back again, and again, and finally lay down, keeping up a steady fire'.

Irish Brigade had five hundred and forty killed or wounded, almost two hundred of whom came from 69th Regiment.

1903: Frank O'Connor, writer, best known for his short stories, born Michael O'Donovan in Cork City. Works include *Guests of the Nation* (1931), *The Saint and Mary Kate* (1932) and *An Only Child* (1961).

1937: Ten young men, ranging in age from 13 to 21 years, died on Scottish farm at Kirkintilloch when their bothy caught fire. The ten, all natives of Achill Island had been employed for season as potato gatherers or 'tatie hokers'.

18/9

1851: Death of Anne Devlin, patriot and heroine.

Usually referred to by historians as 'Robert Emmet's house-keeper', was committed rebel by time she met Emmet and entered into plot in guise of housekeeper. Imprisoned in Kilmainham after botched 1803 rising, suffered severe privation on orders of prison superintendent, Dr Edward Trevor, who locked her away in damp cell, 24 hours a day. Finally released in 1806

Little known about remaining 45 years of life. Died of starvation in Dublin tenement.

1867: 'Manchester Martyrs' ambush.

Richard O'Sullivan Burke organised rescue of leading Fenians, Colonel T.J. Kelly and Captain Timothy Deasy, from prison van in Manchester. Police Sergeant Charles Brett was killed when lock was shot off prison van.

1890: Death in New York of Dion Boucicault, dramatist, actor and man of the theatre. Works include *The Corsican Brothers* (1848) and *The Shaughraun* (1874).

1964: Death of Sean O'Casey, playwright. Works include *The Shadow of a Gunman* (1923), *Juno and the Paycock* (1924) and *The Plough and the Stars* (1926).

19/9

1757: Opening of St Patrick's Hospital, Dublin, built with bequest from Dean Jonathan Swift, to care for the mentally ill.

1880: Speech by Charles Stewart Parnell at Ennis, Co. Clare:

When a man takes a farm from which another has been evicted, you must show him in the streets of the town, you must show him in the fair and in the marketplace, and even in the house of worship, by leaving him severely alone, by putting him into moral Coventry, by isolating him from his kind as if he was a leper of old – You must show him your detestation of the crime he has committed and you may depend upon it that there will be no man so full of avarice, so lost to shame, as to dare the public opinion of all right-thinking men and to transgress your unwritten code of laws.

1905: Death of Dr Thomas John Barnardo, founder of famous children's charity which bears his name.

20/9

1803: 25-year-old Robert Emmet, United Irishman, was hanged at Thomas St, Dublin.

> Let no man write my epitaph; for as no man who knows my motives dares now vindicate them, let not prejudice nor ignorance asperse them. Let them rest in obscurity and peace; my memory be left in oblivion, and my tomb remain uninscribed, until other times and other men can do justice to my character. When my country takes her place among the nations of the earth, then, and not till then, let my epitaph be written.
>
> — Emmet, Speech from the Dock

1847: Michael Cusack, chief founder of GAA (1884), born at Carron, Co. Clare.

1970: Death of Leo Rowsome, renowned 'King of the Irish Pipers'.

21/9

1795: 'The Battle of the Diamond'.

Protestant 'Peep O' Day Boys' routed Catholic 'Defenders' in faction fight near Loughgall, Co. Armagh. Engagement, which left at least thirty Catholics dead, was commemorated that same evening in home of James Sloan, innkeeper of Loughgall, by founding of Orange Society, latterly Orange Order 'to maintain the laws and peace of the Country and the Protestant Constitution, and to defend the King and his heirs as long as they shall maintain the Protestant ascendancy'. As a result of activities of the paramilitary 'Peep O' Day Boys' in the county, an estimated five thousand Co. Armagh Catholics migrated to Mayo and other western counties between 1795 and 1796 – probably greatest displacement of population within Ireland in recent centuries.

1881: Eamonn Ceannt, revolutionary and one of seven signatories of Proclamation of 1916, born at Ballymore, Glenamaddy, Co. Galway.

22/9

1721: Death of Thomas Doggett, comic actor.
Born in Dublin, was a staunch Hanovarian. On 1 August 1716, to honour accession of George I to throne, donated funds for a coat and badge 'to be rowed for by six watermen from London Bridge to Chelsea and to be continued annually on the same day forever'. 'The Doggett Coat and Badge Race' remains oldest annually contested event in British sporting calender.

1884: *HMS Wasp* was wrecked off Tory Island with loss of fifty-two lives.

1957: Death of Oliver St John Gogarty, surgeon, wit and writer. Works include *Poems and Plays* (1920) and *It isn't This Time of Year at All* (1954).

1989: Ten military bandsmen died when Provisional IRA bombed Royal Marine School of Music in Deal, Kent.

23/9

1911: Sir Edward Carson addressed fifty thousand members of Orange Order and Unionist Clubs at Craigavon House.

'We must be prepared ... the morning Home Rule passes, ourselves to become responsible for the government of the Protestant province of Ulster'.

1974: Death of Denis Ireland, author and Nationalist.
Belfast-born Protestant, devoted much of writing to ideal of a United Ireland. 1948, nominated to Seanad Éireann by Taoiseach John A. Costello, becoming first resident of Northern Ireland to become member of Oireachtas.

1992: In Belfast, 2,000-pound IRA bomb destroyed forensic science laboratory on outskirts of city as well as damaging over 700 surrounding houses. Repair costs estimated at £20 million.

24/9

1786: Charles Bianconi, promoter of Irish road-car service, born in Lombardy.

1798: Execution in Dublin of 24-year-old Bartholomew Teeling, General Humbert's aide-de-camp, captured after Battle of Ballinamuck.

1892: Death in St Louis, USA of Patrick Sarsfield Gilmore, bandmaster and composer. Works include 'When Johnny Comes Marching Home'.

25/9

1917: Death on hunger-strike in Mountjoy jail, after being forcibly fed, of 32-year-old Thomas Ashe, patriot.

Achieved only conclusive volunteer victory during Easter Rising, when, with fewer than fifty men in Ashbourne area of Co. Meath, won pitched battle with RIC and captured 4 police barracks, together with large quantities of arms and ammunition.

1983: Break-out from Long Kesh prison of thirty-eight Provisional IRA prisoners, of whom nineteen made good their escape.

26/9

1766: Death of Frances Sheridan (née Chamberlaine), novelist, dramatist and mother of Richard Brinsley Sheridan. Works include *Memoirs of Miss Sidney Biddulph* (1761).

1965: Death of Colonel James C. Fitzmaurice, aviator and co-pilot on first east–west flight across the Atlantic in 1928.

27/9

1764: Death of Henry Boyle, Earl of Shannon, Speaker of Irish House of Commons, 1733–53.

Described by Robert Walpole as 'King of the Irish Commons'. On father's side, was grandson of Lord Braghill who assisted Cromwell in subduing Munster. On mother's side, was grandson of Lord Inchiquin, notorious 'Murrough of the Burnings'. Died of 'gout of in the head'.

1891: Charles Stewart Parnell, Nationalist leader, made his last public appearance and speech at Creggs, Co. Roscommon.

28/9

1889: Seán Keating, landscape and figurative painter, born in Limerick.

1912: Ulster's Solemn League and Covenant was signed.
 While Third Home Rule Bill still being debated at Westminster, Edward Carson led two hundred thousand Orangemen in signing Solemn League and Covenant in Belfast. Pledged Ulstermen to use 'all means which may be found necessary to defeat the present conspiracy to set up a Home Rule parliament in Ireland'. All over Ulster, Unionists signed copies. As many as four hundred thousand signatures were recorded.

1964: In Belfast, 'Tricolour riots' began.
 When, in run-up to 1964 Westminster general election, Sinn Féin candidate for marginal Belfast West constituency, Liam McMillan, mounted tricolour in window of his election headquaters in Divis St, there were complaints and demands that it be removed. Under Flags and Emblems Display Act, passed by Stormont régime in 1954, it was an offence to display tricolour anywhere in Northern Ireland. Forcible removal of flag, by large contingent of RUC in riot gear on 28 September, led to several nights of violent rioting, worst disturbances in Belfast for more than 30 years.

29/9

1778: Catherine McAuley, foundress of Order of Mercy (1831), born in Dublin.

1908: Greer Garson, actress and Academy Award winner, as best actress in title role of *Mrs Miniver* (1942), born in Co. Down.

1922: General Eoin O'Duffy was appointed first Commissioner of Garda Síochána.

1928: Death of John Devoy, Fenian and one of most influential members of Clan Na Gael.

1979: Pope John Paul II arrived in Ireland on 3-day visit – first Pope to step on Irish soil.

On arrival, celebrated Mass in Phoenix Park, Dublin, before a crowd in excess of a million. In major address during Mass at Drogheda later that day, strongly condemned violence and called for conciliation and justice in Ireland. Over following 2 days, visited Maynooth and Clonmacnois and celebrated Mass at Galway, Knock and Limerick.

30/9

1852: Sir Charles Stanford, composer and music teacher whose pupils included Vaughan Williams and Gustav Holst, born in Dublin.

1893: General Seán MacEoin, soldier and politician known as 'Blacksmith of Ballinalee', born at Bunlahy, Granard, Co. Longford.

October

1/10

1795: St Patrick's College, Maynooth, formally opened.

Established by an act of parliament 'for the better education of persons professing the popish or Roman Catholic religion' and endowed with an annual grant of £8,000, rising soon to more than £9,000.

1840: Cardinal Michael Logue, Archbishop of Armagh (1888–1924), born at Carrigart, Co. Donegal.

1843: Daniel O'Connell presided at Repeal meeting attended by estimated four hundred thousand at Mullaghmast, Co. Kildare.

1877: Death of David Moriarty, vehement anti-Fenian Bishop of Kerry from 1856.

When we look down into the fathomless depths of the Fenian conspiracy we must acknowledge that eternity is not long enough nor hell hot enough for such miscreants....
Sermon, February 1867

1917: Cardinal Cahal Daly, Archbishop of Armagh and Primate of All Ireland (1990–), born at Loughguile, Co. Antrim.

2/10

1831: Edwin Lawrence Godkin, editor and author, in honour of whom 'Godkin Lectures' on government were established at Harvard University, born at Mayne, Co. Wicklow.

1852: William O'Brien, Irish Party MP, who, with John Dillon, initiated 'plan of campaign' (1886) to force landlords to reduce exorbitant rents, born in Mallow, Co. Cork.

1942: *Curaçao* disaster.
   British cruiser *Curaçao* sank off Co. Donegal coast with the loss of three hundred and thirty-eight lives, after collision with Cunard liner *Queen Mary*.

1975: In Northern Ireland, twelve people killed and forty-six injured in series of UVF gun and bomb attacks.

   : Death of Seamus Murphy, sculptor and stone-carver.

3/10

1691: Treaty of Limerick signed by Williamite commander, General Ginkel, and Irish commander, Patrick Sarsfield.
   Under military articles of Treaty some 12,000 Irish troops eventually enlisted in armies of Louis XIV of France to become known as the 'Wild Geese'.

1750: 26-year-old James MacLaine, or McLean, gentleman highwayman, was executed at Tyburn.
   Born in Monaghan in 1724, was arrested and sent for trial at Old Bailey in July 1750. In his lodgings were found 23 purses, a quantity of clothes and, 'a famous kept mistress'. Arrest caused great excitement and many great ladies 'shedded tears in abundance' at his trial. On one particular day no less than three thousand people visited condemned Irishman in his cell at Newgate, with the crush so great that he fainted twice.

1971: Death, aged 40, of Seán Ó Riada, composer and musician who founded Ceoltóirí Chualann in 1961.

4/10

1886: Lennox Robinson, playwright and manager of Abbey Theatre (1910–23), born in Douglas in Cork. Works include *The Clancy Name* (1908) and *The White Blackbird* (1925).

1969: Death of Cathal O'Shannon, trade unionist and journalist.

5/10

1911: Brian O'Nolan, author and newspaper columnist, alias Myles Na gCopaleen and Flann O'Brien, born in Strabane, Co. Tyrone. Works include *At-Swim-Two-Birds* (1939) and *An Béal Bocht* (1941).

1968: Northern Ireland Civil Rights Association (NICRA) march in Derry.

Over one hundred injured when march, banned by Stormont Minister of Home Affairs, William Craig, was brutally dispersed by RUC. Extensive media coverage of police action did much to accelerate demise of Stormont régime.

6/10

1891: Death in Brighton, aged 45, of Charles Stewart Parnell, Nationalist leader.

Years later, Katharine O'Shea vividly recalled exact moment of great leader's passing:

> Late in the evening he suddenly opened his eyes and said; 'Kiss me, sweet wifie, and I will try to sleep a little'. I lay down by his side and kissed the burning lips he pressed to mine for the last time. The fire of them, fierce beyond any that I had ever felt, even in his most loving moods, startled me, and as I slipped my hand from under his head he gave a little sigh and became unconscious. The doctor came at once, but no remedies prevailed against this sudden failure of the heart's action and my husband died without regaining consciousness, before his last kiss was cold on my lips.

1928: Death, aged 45, of Pádraic Ó Conaire, writer in the Irish language. Works include *An Chéad Chloch* (1914) and *M'Asal Beag Dubh* (1944).

7/10

1843: Lord Lieutenant proclaimed Daniel O'Connell's proposed 'monster meeting' at Clontarf, scheduled for following day.

Meeting at Clontarf, intended to be last and biggest in a

series of 'monster meetings' in support of repeal of Act of Union was subsequently cancelled by O'Connell. A week later, he was arrested on a charge of conspiracy.

1982: Death of Séamus Ennis, celebrated Irish uilleann piper and collector of airs.

8/10

1889: Margaret Burke Sheridan, opera singer, born at Castlebar, Co. Mayo.

Personally coached by great Giacomo Puccini. Subsequently became one of Puccini's great interpreters, endearing herself to Italian opera-loving public who gave her pet-name of 'The Irish Butterfly'. Made only one major appearance in Ireland – at the Theatre Royal in Dublin in 1922.

1949: Death of Edith Œnone Somerville, literary partner of Violet Martin (Martin Ross). Works include *The Real Charlotte* (1894) and *Some Experiences of an Irish R.M.* (1899).

9/10

1974: Death of Padraic Fallon, poet and playwright. Works include *Diarmuid and Gráinne* (1953) and *The Vision of Mac Conglinne* (1953).

10/10

1790: Fr Theobald Mathew, temperance campaigner, born at Thomastown Castle, Cashel, Co. Tipperary.

1918: City of Dublin's steam-packet company's *RMS Leinster* was sunk by German torpedoes just one hour out of Dún Laoghaire harbour.

Of seven hundred and seventy-one on board, five hundred and one, mainly soldiers returning from leave, went down with ship.

1922: Catholic hierarchy delivered clearly unambiguous pastoral letter on Civil War:

... a section of the community, refusing to acknowledge the government set up by the nation, have chosen to attack their own country as if she were a foreign power ... They carry on what they call a war, but which in the absence of any legitimate authority to justify it, is morally only a system of murder and assassination of the National Forces....

11/10

1921: Anglo–Irish Peace Conference opened in London.

Irish delegation comprised Arthur Griffith, Michael Collins, Robert Barton, Eamonn Duggan and George Gavan Duffy.

1932: In Northern Ireland, government banned marches under Special Powers Act.

Ban followed a week of conflict in Belfast between police and unemployed workers seeking higher payments under Outdoor Relief Scheme. During protest, workers from both sides of religious divide paraded to Custom House, led by Catholic and Protestant bands, who, to avoid giving religious offence to one another, repeatedly played neutral tune 'Yes, We Have No Bananas'. Increases in outdoor relief were granted some days later.

1969: Death of Louise Gavan Duffy, revolutionary, and founder, in 1917, of Scoil Bhríde, first all-Irish school for girls in Dublin.

12/10

1865: Death in France of William Wallace, Waterford-born composer. Compositions include operas *Maritana* (1845) and *Lurline* (1860).

1876: Jerome Connor, sculptor, born at Coomduff, Annascaul, Co. Kerry.

1975: Canonisation of Oliver Plunkett, Archbishop of Armagh (1669–81).

Beatified in 1920, was first Irishman to be made a saint since Laurence O'Toole in 1226.

1984: IRA bomb exploded in Grand Hotel Brighton, during Conservative Party Conference.

Five died, including an MP and the wife of the government

chief whip, and a further thirty were injured. Prime Minister, Mrs Thatcher, who was in hotel at time, was uninjured.

13/10

1864: Death of William Pembroke Mulchinock, poet who wrote 'The Rose of Tralee'.

1981: Death of Oisín Kelly, sculptor, whose works include statue of James Larkin in O'Connell St, Dublin.

14/10

1791: First Society of United Irishmen established in Belfast by Wolfe Tone, Henry Joy McCracken, Thomas Russell and Samuel Neilson.

Objectives were 'to abolish all unnatural religious distinctions, to unite all Irishmen against the unjust influence of Great Britain, and secure their true representation in a national Parliament'. Initially, United Irishmen were reformers rather than revolutionaries. 1795, society reformed as secret, revolutionary organisation.

1797: William Orr, United Irishman, was hanged at Carrickfergus, Co. Antrim.

Convicted by packed jury on charge of administering treasonable oath to two soldiers. Execution aroused widespread public indignation as he was popularly thought to have been innocent.

1814: Thomas Davis, poet, Nationalist and co-founder of *The Nation* newspaper (1842), born at Mallow, Co. Cork, son of British army surgeon.

1817: Death of John Philpot Curran, lawyer and father of Sarah Curran.

1882: Eamon De Valera, revolutionary, politician, and third President of Ireland, born in New York.

Son of Catherine Coll from Knockmore, Bruree, Co. Limerick and Vivian Juan De Valera, Spaniard whose father was engaged in sugar trade between Cuba, Spain and United States.

1920: Seán Treacy, celebrated IRA Volunteer, shot dead by British troops in Talbot St, Dublin.

1928: The Gate Theatre, founded by Hilton Edwards and Micheál MacLíammóir, opened in Dublin.
Opened with production of *Peer Gynt*, involving cast of forty-eight before capacity audience of one hundred and two.

1958: Death of Lennox Robinson, playwright associated with Abbey Theatre. Works include *The Whiteheaded Boy* (1916) and *Drama at Inish* (1933).

15/10

1763: Lord Edward FitzGerald, United Irishman, born at Carton House, Co. Kildare, twelfth child of first Duke of Leinster.

1842: First edition of *The Nation* newspaper.
Founded by Thomas Davis, John Blake Dillon and Charles Gavan Duffy. Aim was 'to create and foster public opinion in Ireland and make it racy of the soil'.

1945: Death of Eoin MacNeill, scholar, patriot and politician.

16/10
Feast of St Gall, Apostle of Switzerland

1588: Fr Luke Wadding, Franciscan scholar whose massive history of Franciscan Order, *Annales Ordinis Minorum* (8 vols, 1625–54) earned him an international reputation, born in Waterford.

1854: Oscar Fingal O'Flahertie Wills Wilde, poet, wit and dramatist, born in Dublin, younger son of surgeon and antiquary Sir William Wilde and Jane Francesca Elgee, 'Speranza' of *The Nation*. Works include *The Picture of Dorian Gray* (1891) and *The Ballad of Reading Gaol* (1898).

1890: Michael Collins, revolutionary leader, born at Woodfield, Clonakilty, Co. Cork, last of eight children of small farmer.

1988: Ireland won Dunhill Nations Golf Cup at St Andrew's.
  Represented by Eamonn Darcy, Des Smyth and Ronan Rafferty. Victory was finest team success in Irish sport since Christy O'Connor and Harry Bradshaw won Canada Cup in 1958. Irish team of David Feherty, Ronan Rafferty and Philip Walton repeated feat in 1990.

17/10

1803: William Smith O'Brien, Young Irelander, born at Drumoland, Co. Clare.

1860: Roderic O'Conor, first and greatest Irish impressionist painter, born at Milltown, Co. Roscommon.

1873: Death of Robert McClure, explorer.
  Born in Wexford, is credited with discovering North-West Passage. Stretch of sea between Victoria and Melville Islands in Arctic Ocean is named after him as the McClure Straights.

18/10

c.1714: Margaret 'Peg' Woffington, celebrated actress on London stage, born in Dublin.

1970: Death of Máirtín Ó Cadhain, scholar, Republican and writer. Works include *Cré Na Cille* (1949).

19/10

1745: Death of Jonathan Swift, poet, pamphleteer, satirist and author.
  In later years, was severely afflicted by deafness, and lived in constant terror of losing his mind. Spirits never recovered from loss of his beloved Stella – the beautiful Hester Johnson – his lifelong companion who died in 1728.
  Despite his infirmities, still managed to keep up regular correspondence with English associates such as Pope and Arbuthnot. Popularity too remained as great as ever. Fury against English misrule in Ireland, vented in celebrated series of letters and pamphlets, had made him a hero among Dublin poor. Had only to stand outside deanery to view one of worst slums in Europe.

In 1742, lapsed into state of dementia, and, for last 3 years of his life was known to speak only once or twice. Died in his seventy-eighth year, leaving, in what he himself described as a satiric touch, £8,000 to build a home for the insane.

1989: The Guildford Four – Paul Hill, Carole Richardson, Gerard Conlon and Patrick Armstrong – were released from prison, having served 15 years of life sentences for their alleged involvement in Provisional IRA bombings in Britain in 1974. Court of Appeal quashed their convictions.

1991: In cycling, Seán Kelly won the Tour of Lombardy.

20/10

1674: James Logan, colonial statesman and scholar, born in Lurgan, Co. Armagh.

Son of a Quaker schoolmaster, became secretary to William Penn and sailed with him to Pennsylvania in 1699. Thereafter had distinguished career in the territory, becoming Chief Justice of Supreme Court in 1731. Made fortune from land investment and trade with Indians and lived in opulent style on 500-acre estate at Germantown near Philadelphia. Devoted later years to study of natural science and botany.

1870: Death of Michael William Balfe, violinist, singer and composer. Compositions include *The Bohemian Girl* (1843).

21/10

1803: 35-year-old Thomas Russell, United Irishman immortalised in Florence M. Wilson's poem 'The Man From God Knows Where', was hanged for high treason at Downpatrick, Co. Down.

1879: Irish National Land League founded in Dublin by Michael Davitt, Charles Stewart Parnell, Thomas Brennan and Patrick Egan.

1904: Patrick Kavanagh, poet, born at Inniskeen, Co. Monaghan, son of a small farmer. Works include *The Great Hunger* (1942) and *Tarry Flynn* (1948).

1906: Death of Colonel E.J. Saunderson, leader of Irish Unionist Party since 1886.

1917: The poet W.B. Yeats, aged 52, married George Hyde-Lees, aged 26.

22/10

1935: Death of Edward Carson, first Baron Carson of Duncairn, lawyer, politician and leader of Ulster Unionists (1910–21).

1966: George Blake, British KGB agent serving 42-year sentence for spying, escaped from Wormwood Scrubs prison in daring operation organised by Limerickman Seán Bourke.

1976: Cearbhall Ó Dálaigh, fifth President of Ireland, resigned.
    A few days earlier Minister for Defence, Patrick Donegan had reportedly referred to President as 'a thundering disgrace' for referring Emergency Powers Bill to Supreme Court to test its constitutionality. Ó Dálaigh resigned so as 'to protect the dignity and independence of the Presidency as an institution'.

23/10

1641: Rising in Ulster began.
    In early days of rebellion, estimated twelve thousand Protestant men, women and children were either killed or died of their privations.

24/10

1854: Sir Horace Plunkett, pioneer of agricultural co-operation born in Gloucestershire, England.

1920: Death on seventy-fourth day of his hunger-strike in Brixton prison of Terence MacSwiney, revolutionary and Lord Mayor of Cork.

1990: In Northern Ireland, six soldiers and one civilian died in Provisional IRA bomb-attacks on security checkpoints near Derry and Newry.

25/10

1899: Micheál MacLíammóir, actor, writer and man of the theatre, born in Cork.

Won wide acclaim through such performances as Robert Emmet in *The Old Lady Says No* (1929), as Heathcliff in *Wuthering Heights*, but particularly through legendary performances as Hamlet.

In early years, had considerable success as a painter. Studied Nijinsky and the Ballets Russes: ballet his favourite art form. Works include 11 full-length plays, both in Irish and English and 5 volumes of autobiography. In 1928 he co-founded both Taibhdhearc na Gaillimhe – Irish-speaking theatre – and the Gate Theatre in Dublin.

Greatest theatrical success in 1960 with his one-man entertainment *The Importance of Being Oscar*, which won him international acclaim.

1960: Death of Harry Ferguson, engineer and inventor.

26/10

1588: The *Girona* of the Spanish Armada was wrecked off Lacada Point, Port na Spánaigh, Co. Antrim.

A 700-ton Neapolitan galleass, it had left Killybegs, Co. Donegal 3 days earlier with thirteen hundred men on board. Only nine survivors. Some 12,000 artefacts have been recovered from wreck, most extensive collection of relics of Armada's presence in Irish waters.

1771: John MacKenna, Chilean general, born at Clogher, Co. Tyrone.

27/10

1919: James Joseph Magennis, Northern Ireland's only Victoria Cross winner of Second World War, born in Belfast.

Magennis won his VC as 'the first and only frogman to work against an enemy from a midget submarine and the first and only frogman … ever to leave a boat under an enemy ship and attach limpet mines' during royal navy attack on Japanese cruiser *Takao* off Singapore in July 1945.

In 1952, Magennis so hard-up that he was obliged to sell his VC for a paltry £75. However, a well-wisher bought the medal back and returned it to him on condition that he never sold it again. Shortly after his death, in 1986, his Victoria Cross fetched £31,900 at auction.

1947: Death of William Fay, actor, producer and co-founder of Abbey Theatre.

28/10

1927: Sixteen fishermen, nine of whom were from island of Inishbofin, were drowned off Cleggan, Co. Galway.

1931: Death in Adelaide, Australia of Patrick MacMahon Glynn, lawyer and politician.

Born in Gort, Co. Galway, elected MP for West Adelaide in South Australian parliament in 1887 and to new Commonwealth parliament in Melbourne in 1901. Subsequently became attorney-general (1909), minister for external affairs (1913) and minister for home and territories (1917).

1955: Death of Sir Arthur Du Cross, Dublin-born pioneer of pneumatic tyre industry and founder of multinational Dunlop Rubber Company (1901).

29/10

1816: Death of Arthur O'Neill, 'Last of the Itinerant Harpers'.

Born at Drumnaslea, Dungannon, Co. Tyrone, blind from childhood. Spent life travelling from one great house to another throughout Ireland, always welcomed as honoured guest. Most distinguished musician present at Belfast Harp Festival of 1792.

Unlike most of his fellow musicians, careful about personal appearance and dress. Large silver buttons on his long coat bore Hand of Ulster, emblem of the O'Neills. Despite his blindness , skilled at both cards and backgammon.

Died aged 89, leaving comprehensive 'memoirs' to posterity.

30/10

1751: Richard Brinsley Sheridan, orator and playwright, born in Dublin. Works include *The Rivals* (1775), *The School for Scandal* (1777) and *The Critic* (1779).

1892: General Eoin O'Duffy, first commissioner of Civic Guard, Garda Síochána (1922), born near Castleblaney, Co. Monaghan.

31/10

1838: Sir William Francis Butler, soldier and author, born at Suirville, Co. Tipperary. Works include *The Great Lone Land* (1872), based on his experiences as British soldier in Canada

1867: Death of William Parsons, third Earl of Rosse.
      1842–5, constructed in grounds of Birr Castle, what was, until 1917, world's largest reflecting telescope. Telescope, which consisted of a 6-foot long reflector in a tube 56 feet long and 7 feet in diameter, raised between two 50-foot walls, was product of 17 years labour and cost £20,000 to construct.

November

1/11

1625: St Oliver Plunkett, Archbishop of Armagh and martyr, born at Loughcrew, Co. Meath.

1884: Gaelic Athletic Association (GAA), with aim of preserving and promoting national pastimes, founded at meeting in Hayes' Commercial Hotel, Thurles, Co. Tipperary.

1920: 18-year-old IRA Volunteer Kevin Barry hanged in Mountjoy jail.
    A medical student, he was executed for murder of an even younger British soldier during IRA raid in Dublin the previous September. First IRA Volunteer to be executed by British authorities during War of Independence.

    : James Daley executed in the Punjab, India
    From Tyrrelspass, Co. Westmeath, one of fourteen soldiers of Connaught Rangers sentenced to death in wake of 'Connaught Rangers Mutiny'. Had refused to soldier 'in protest against British atrocities in Ireland'. Remaining thirteen had sentences commuted to life imprisonment.

2/11

1797: Tyrone Power, actor and playwright, born at Kilmacthomas, Co. Waterford. Works include *The Lost Heir* (1830) and *The King's Secret* (1831).

1800: Death of Thomas Whaley or Whalley, Dublin-born politician and playwright, known as 'Buck' or 'Jerusalem'

Whaley, who once won substantial bet by walking to Jerusalem and back to Dublin.

1950: Death, aged 94, of George Bernard Shaw, playwright and Nobel Prize for Literature winner (1925). Works include *Man and Superman* (1903) and *Pygmalion* (1913).

3/11

1815: John Mitchel, patriot, born at Dungiven, Co. Derry, son of Presbyterian minister.

1917: Conor Cruise O'Brien, academic, diplomat and writer, born in Dublin. Works include *Maria Cross* (1953) and *To Katanga and Back* (1962).

1923: Cardinal Tomás Ó Fiaich, Archbishop of Armagh and Primate of All-Ireland (1977–90), born at Anamar, Crossmaglen, Co. Armagh.

1932: Albert Reynolds, Leader of Fianna Fáil and Taoiseach (1992–) born at Rooskey, Co. Roscommon.

4/11
Feast of St Malachy, Archbishop of Armagh
Malachy – Mael Maedoc – died in 1148; canonised by Pope Clement III in 1190 – first papal canonisation of an Irishman.

So-called 'Prophecies of St Malachy', describing popes from twelfth-century Celestine II 'to the end of the world', are accurate enough until 1590 but extremely vague after that. Since they were unheard of before that year it is believed that they were forged by a candidate at Papal conclave of that year to support his aspirations.

1884: Harry Ferguson, engineer and inventor, notably of Ferguson tractor, born at Growell, Hillsborough, Co. Down.

5/11
1798: Death of John Holwell, survivor of 'Black Hole of Calcutta'. Dublin-born Holwell amongst mere twenty-three survivors

of hundred and forty-six British subjects imprisoned overnight in Nawab of Bengal's notorious chamber. Subsequently wrote colourful account of incident, which fuelled considerable anti-Indian feeling in Britain when published in 1758, and continued to do so for over a century afterwards.

Became public hero in Britain and later succeeded Robert Clive as Governor of Bengal. Spent last years writing on Indian history and religion.

6/11

1649: Death of Owen Roe O'Neill, general and nephew of Hugh O'Neill, Earl of Tyrone.

Professional soldier in army of Spain until 1642 when he returned to Ireland to take command over fellow Ulstermen who had risen in rebellion. Greatest success came in June 1646 at Benburb where he practically annihilated superior force of Scots parliamentarians under General Robert Monroe. Victory, however, had little bearing on subsequent events. Planters soon afterwards gained initiative and by August 1649 Cromwell had landed. Owen Roe making his way south to join Ormond and royalist army when he died at Cloughoughter Castle, Co. Cavan. There is a tradition that he was poisoned by enemy agents.

1963: Death, aged 99, of Daniel Mannix, Archbishop of Melbourne and leading figure in Australian Catholic hierarchy for over half a century.

7/11

1878: Margaret Cousins, teacher and worker for women's rights in India, where she became first woman magistrate, born Margaret Gillespie in Boyle, Co. Roscommon.

1881: Death of John MacHale, Archbishop of Tuam, and dominant figure in Catholic hierarchy during middle decades of nineteenth century.

1980: Death, aged 91, of Frank Duff, chief founder of Legion of Mary (1921).

8/11

1847: Abraham 'Bram' Stoker, writer of classic horror tale *Dracula* (1897), born in Dublin.

1960: Niemba ambush, the Congo (now Zaïre).

Nine Irish UN soldiers died when platoon from 33rd Infantry Battalion, led by Lieutenant Kevin Gleeson, was ambushed by Baluba tribesmen. To date (1993), seventy-seven Irishmen have died while serving with UN peace-keeping forces – of these, twenty-six died in the Congo/Zaïre.

1987: Remembrance Day massacre, Enniskillen, Co. Fermanagh.

Eleven Protestant civilians, including three elderly married couples and a 20-year-old nurse, killed and a further sixty injured when bomb exploded without warning during Remembrance Day parade in the town. Provisional IRA claimed responsibility saying that bomb was intended for Crown forces.

9/11

1875: Sir Hugh Lane, art collector and critic, born in Ballybrack, Co. Cork.

1892: Death of Patrick W. Nally, athlete and Fenian.

1926: Hugh Leonard, pseudonym of John Keyes Byrne, author, scriptwriter and playwright, born in Dalkey, Co. Dublin. Works include *Da* (1973) and *A Life* (1979).

1935: Arranmore, Co. Donegal, boating tragedy.

Nineteen drowned when boat struck rocks off Arranmore Island. Twelve of victims were islanders returning from Scotland where they had been harvesting potatoes.

10/11

1580: Massacre at Dun an Óir, Ballyferriter, Co. Kerry.

Massacre of garrison at Dun an Óir, small promontory fort, was one of bloodiest episodes of Elizabethan wars in Ireland. Over six hundred men, women and children – Spanish, Italian and Irish – coldbloodedly slaughtered after they had surrendered to Lord Deputy Grey and Sir Walter Raleigh. It was, in the words of Seán O'Faolain 'one of those incidents in history which, though politically slight and unimportant in themselves, will never be forgotten'.

1728: Oliver Goldsmith, author, born at Pallas, Co. Longford, son of a clergyman. Works include *The Vicar of Wakefield* (1766). and 'The Deserted Village' (1770).

1832: Charles Russell, Baron Russell of Killowen, barrister who, in 1894, became Lord Chief Justice of England – first Catholic to be appointed to the position since Reformation – born in Newry, Co. Down.

1841: Death of Catherine McAuley, foundress of Order of Mercy (1831).

1879: Patrick Henry Pearse, educationalist, writer and revolutionary, born in Dublin. Works include *The Murder Machine* (1912) and *An Mháthair agus Sgéalta Eile* (1916).

1966: Seán Lemass resigned as Taoiseach and leader of Fianna Fáil. Succeeded by Jack Lynch.

11/11

1880: Ned Kelly, Australian bushranger, hanged in Melbourne.

Only Australian bushranger to become folk-hero. Son of 'Red Kelly' who was transported from Tipperary for attempting to shoot a landlord. Reared in foothills of Northern Victoria where, on his father's death, his mother turned their hut into a shanty house which in time became centre for army of bandits who conducted a sporadic war against their better-off neighbours.

Irish sense of injustice was aimed principally at police. A policeman was a man who 'for a lazy, loafing, cowardly billet left the ash corner, deserted the shamrock, the emblem of true wit and beauty to serve under a flag and nation as has destroyed, massacred and murdered their forefathers by the greatest of tortures'.

Still only in his mid-twenties, tracked down, mainly by Irish policemen. Last words on mounting gallows were 'Such is life'.

1918: First World War ended.

An estimated 49,000 Irishmen gave their lives in the conflict.

12/11

1872: William Fay, actor and theatrical producer with his elder brother, Frank, born in Dublin.

1964: Death of Robert Brennan, diplomat and author. Works include his autobiography, *Allegiance* (1950).

13/11

1712: Death of Sir William Robinson, architect whose work includes Royal Hospital, Kilmainham, built between 1680 and 1684.

1817: Death of John Keogh, leading Emancipationist and leader of radical section of Catholic Committee in 1790s.

14/11
Feast of St Laurence O'Toole, Archbishop of Dublin (1162–80)

1622: Death of Miler Magrath, clergyman.
Born in Co. Fermanagh, began ecclesiastical career as Franciscan friar and, in 1565, as result of dubious solicitations made in Rome, was elevated to see of Down and Conor. 1567, professed himself a Protestant and was duly rewarded with bishoprics of Emly and Cashel. 1580, after 9 years as both Papal bishop and Anglican archbishop, Pope relieved him of Down and Conor for 'heresy and many other crimes'. Later, after complaining of poverty, was given sees of Waterford and Lismore but subsequently lost them for negligence in providing religious services. Instead was given poorer sees of Killala and Achonry. Died approaching his hundredth birthday.

1827: Death, in New York, of Thomas Addis Emmet, United Irishman, lawyer and elder brother of Robert Emmet.

1918: Death of Seamus O'Kelly, journalist and writer. Works include *The Weaver's Grave* (published posthumously, 1920).
Born in Loughrea, Co. Galway, died suddenly after pro-British mob gate-crashed office at Harcourt St, Dublin. At the

time he was in charge of Arthur Griffith's paper, *Nationality*.

1992: In Belfast, three Catholic men killed and over a dozen injured when Loyalist gunmen attacked bookmaker's shop on Oldpark Road.

15/11

1821: Death of John Barrett, academic and eccentric.

Born at Ballyroan, Co. Laois, in 1753, was Professor of Oriental Languages at Trinity College and vice-provost from 1807. During last 50 years of life, rarely left precincts of college. Instead, confined himself to garret where, allowing himself no fire, even in coldest weather, devoted himself to his passions – reading and hoarding money. On his death, left £80,000 'to feed the hungry and clothe the naked'.

1849: James O'Neill, actor and father of dramatist Eugene O'Neill, born in Kilkenny.

Most famous role was that of Edmond Dantes in stage version of *The Count of Monte Cristo*. Played part more than 6,000 times.

1881: William Pearse, younger brother of Patrick Pearse, both of whom were executed after 1916 Rising, born in Dublin.

1985: Anglo–Irish Agreement was signed.

Otherwise known as Hillsborough Agreement, document on structures for the government of Northern Ireland was signed at Hillsborough Castle, Co. Down by Taoiseach, Dr Garret FitzGerald and British prime minister, Margaret Thatcher.

16/11

1733: Death of Sir Edward Lovett Pearce, architect who designed the Parliament House in College Green, Dublin.

1965: Death of W.T. (William Thomas) Cosgrave, first President of the Executive Council of the Irish Free State (1922–32).

1986: Death of Siobhán McKenna, leading lady of modern Irish theatre.

17/11

1875: Death of Charles Vignoles, civil engineer and international railway consultant.

1974: Death of Erskine Hamilton Childers, fourth President of Ireland (from May 1973).

18/11

1880: Irish Football Association (IFA) was formed.

1889: Death of William Allingham, poet, known as 'The Bard of Ballyshannon'. Collections include *Day and Night Songs* (1854).

1982: Death of Hilton Edwards, co-founder of Gate Theatre, Dublin.

19/11

1798: Death, aged 35, of Theobald Wolfe Tone, United Irishman renowned as 'Father of Irish Republicanism'.

> To subvert the tyranny of our execrable government, to break the connection with England, the never-failing source of all our political evils and to assert the independence of my country – these were my objects. To unite the whole people of Ireland, to abolish the memory of all past dissensions and to substitute the common name of Irishman in place of the denominations of Protestant, Catholic and Dissenter – these were my means.

(Autobiography)

1913: Irish Citizen Army founded by James Larkin and James Connolly.

> Establishment of a worker's defence corps to enable workers during Dublin Lock-Out defend themselves in clashes with police was suggested by ex-army officer, Captain J.R. White. Tiny force of about two hundred men, almost disappeared when men returned to work in spring 1914. Later that year, revived by then general labourer Seán O'Casey, and subsequently played a key role in 1916 Rising.

1821: Rockite outrage, Co. Tipperary.
Seventeen people at Shea home in Tubber, near Slievenamon, Co. Tipperary were burnt to death, believed to be victims of Rockite, peasant agitators.

1924: Death of Cardinal Michael Logue, Archbishop of Armagh since 1888.

20/11

1719: Spranger Barry, romantic actor and rival to David Garrick on London stage, born in Dublin.

1983: In Northern Ireland, 'Darkley Massacre' took place.
Breakaway group of INLA entered church of Mountain Lodge Pentecostal Assembly in Darkley, Co. Armagh, and opened fire on congregation. Three Church elders killed.

21/11

1767: Thomas Russell, United Irishman, born at Betsborough, Kilshanick, Co. Cork.
The 'Man From God Knows Where' was Wolfe Tone's closest friend. A founder of United Irishmen and a key figure in its transformation into first Irish republican movement.

1844: William Martin Murphy, founder of Independent Newspapers, born at Bantry, Co. Cork.

1920: 'Bloody Sunday' in Dublin.
'I found that those fellows we put on the spot were going to put a lot of us on the spot, so I got there first'. (Michael Collins)
At around 9 a.m. an IRA 'squad' organised by Collins entered houses and hotels in various parts of Dublin and executed fourteen British secret service agents. That afternoon, Black and Tans killed twelve civilians during Dublin–Tipperary football match at Croke Park, including a player, Michael Hogan of Tipperary. That evening, three prisoners – Dick McKee, Peadar Clancy and Conor Clune – executed by Auxiliaries in Dublin Castle.

1974: Birmingham Pub Bombings.

Twenty-one died and a hundred and sixty-one were injured when Provisional IRA bombs exploded in two Birmingham city centre pubs. August 1975, six Irishmen convicted and given life sentences for bombings. 1987, British Court of Appeal upheld convictions. Men finally released, on third appeal, almost 17 years after sentencing, in March 1991.

22/11

1773: Lord John George Beresford, Archbishop of Armagh and Primate of Ireland (1822–62), born in Dublin.

1912: Donagh MacDonagh, poet, dramatist and son of executed 1916 leader Thomas MacDonagh, born in Dublin.

1963: John Fitzgerald Kennedy, thirty-fifth President of United States, assassinated in Dallas, Texas.

23/11
Feast of St Columbanus, missionary

1867: Execution of 'Manchester Martyrs'.
William Philip Allen, Michael Larkin and Michael O'Brien executed at Salford jail, Manchester, for murder of Sergeant Charles Brett during rescue of Fenians T.J. Kelly and Timothy Deasy in the city that September.

1958: In golf, Ireland, represented by Christy O'Connor and Harry Bradshaw, won Canada Cup.

1963: Death of Patrick MacGill, writer. Works include *Children of the Dead End* (1914) and *The Glen of Carra* (1934).

1966: Death of Seán T. Ó Ceallaigh, second President of Ireland, (1945–59).

1974: Death, in New York, of Cornelius Ryan, war-correspondent and bestselling author. Works include *The Longest Day* (1959) and *A Bridge Too Far* (1974).

24/11

1713: Laurence Sterne, writer, born in Clonmel, Co. Tipperary. Works include *Tristram Shandy* (1759–67) and *Sermon of Mr Yorrick* (1760).

1922: Robert Erskine Childers, patriot and author, executed by Free State authorities. Works include *The Framework of Home Rule* (1911) and *The Constructive Works of Dáil Éireann* (1921).

1940: Death of James Craig, Lord Craigavon, first Prime Minister of Northern Ireland (1921–40).

25/11

1892: Lecture by Douglas Hyde in Leinster Hall, Dublin, 'On the necessity for de-Anglicising the Irish People':

> It has always been very curious to me how Irish sentiment sticks in this half-way house – how it continues to apparently hate the English and at the same time continues to imitate them.

1913: Irish Volunteer movement launched at public meeting at Rotunda Rink in Dublin.

1942: Death of Peadar Kearney, song-writer. Works include Irish national anthem, 'A Soldier's Song' (1907).

26/11

1791: First convicts, sent directly from Ireland, arrived in penal colony of Botany Bay on board the *Queen*.
    1791–1853, some forty thousand Irishmen and women transported to British-administered penal colonies in New South Wales and Western Australia, for terms ranging from 7 years to life. Though sizeable proportion were Irish patriots – United Irishmen, Young Irelanders – vast majority, of whom a quarter were women, sent over for ordinary, petty crime. From outset, showed more rebellious spirit than other convicts. Only two convict mutinies were manned by Irishmen, at Vinegar Hill outside Sydney in 1804, and Norfolk Island in 1834.
    Of Ireland's two million famine emigrants, only seventy

thousand settled in Australia. In 1850s and 1860s, however, convicts and descendants were joined by first real mass migration to Australia. Of estimated third of a million Irish who settled there in nineteenth century, over a hundred thousand lured by assisted passage, arrived 1851–60. Majority were women who travelled in what became known as 'bride ships', bound almost in their entirety for domestic service. In the main from particular counties especially Kilkenny, Tipperary, East Limerick, East Clare and North Cork.

Unlike Irish emigrants to United States who concentrated in cities such as Boston, New York and Chicago, compatriots in Australia formed cohesive groups over a wide range of areas. As a result, today's estimated six million Australians of Irish extraction – 30% of population – widely spread throughout the country.

1872: Osborn Bergin, Gaelic scholar, born in Cork.

1910: Cyril Cusack, stage and screen actor, born in Durban, South Africa.

27/11

1857: Thomas Heazle Parke, surgeon and traveller, born at Drumsna, Carrick-on-Shannon, Co. Leitrim.

1878: Sir William Orpen, portrait, landscape and genre painter, born at Stillorgan, Co. Dublin.

1906: Death of Michael Cusack, chief-founder of GAA (1884).

1969: Death of Séamus Ó Grianna, Gaelic novelist and short-story writer under nom-de-plume, Máire. Works include *Caisleáin Óir* (1924), *Cith is Dealán* (1926) and *Nuair a Bhí mé Óg* (1942).

28/11

1856: Cardinal Patrick O'Donnell, Archbishop of Armagh (1924–7) born at Kilraine, Glenties, Co. Donegal.

1871: Gaiety Theatre, Dublin, opened with production of Goldsmith's *She Stoops to Conquer*.

1905: Sinn Féin political movement launched by Arthur Griffith at convention in Dublin.

Name 'Sinn Féin', meaning 'Ourselves', coined by Máire Butler, cousin of Unionist leader, Sir Edward Carson. Convention adopted resolution: 'That the people of Ireland are a free people, and that no law made without their authority or consent is, or can ever be, binding on their conscience'.

1920: At Kilmichael, Co. Cork, eighteen-man Auxiliary patrol wiped out by IRA flying column under General Tom Barry.

29/11

1853: John Mitchel concluded his *Jail Journal*.

Jail Journal, published in 1854, has been variously described as 'a classic in prison literature', 'the greatest literary achievement of Irish nationalism' and as 'a book, unparalleled in Irish history, in the amount of evil it accomplished'.

30/11

1667: Jonathan Swift, Dean of St Patrick's Cathedral and writer, born in Dublin. Works include *The Battle of the Books* (1697), *Conduct of the Allies* (1711) and *Gulliver's Travels* (1726).

1900: Death, aged 46, in Paris, of Oscar Wilde, wit and dramatist.

Social outcast after imprisonment for homosexuality, lived last 18 months of life in complete poverty, spending much of lonely time writing letters, mostly about money worries.

Initially buried in pauper's grave in Bagneux. 1909, remains moved to Père Lachaise cemetery where a winged angel guards his tomb.

1944: Death of General Eoin O'Duffy.

Chief-of-staff of IRA (1922), first commissioner, at age of 30, of Garda Síochána (1922), leader of 'National Guard' or 'Blueshirts' (1933) and first president of Fine Gael Party (1933).

1967: Death of Patrick Kavanagh, one of Ireland's greatest poets. Works include *The Green Fool* (1938), *The Great Hunger* (1942) and *Tarry Flynn* (1948).

December

1722: Death of Susanna Centlivre, playwright.

Born in Co. Tyrone, wrote a number of highly successful comedies, including *The Wonder: A Woman Keeps A Secret* (1714), which provided David Garrick with one of his best parts. Died, aged 55, 'the lustre of her beauty scarcely touched by time'.

1901: Death in New York of Thomas Clarke Luby, co-founder of Irish Republican Brotherhood or Fenian Movement (1858).

1956: At Olympic Games in Melbourne, Ronnie Delaney of Ireland won gold medal in 1,500 metres event.

1991: Death of Dr Pat O'Callaghan, Irish Olympic hammer-throwing champion (1928, 1932).

1791: Death of Henry Flood, statesman and orator.

Leader of opposition in Irish House of Commons during 1860s, regarded as finest orator of his day. Later replaced by comparatively moderate Henry Grattan, with whom he split after celebrated verbal exchange on floor of House in October 1783.

1805: William Thompson, naturalist, whose *Natural History of Ireland* (1849–56) became the standard work on the subject, born in Belfast.

1811: The Society for Promoting the Education of the Poor in Ireland, better known as Kildare Place Society, founded to organise non-denominational schools in Ireland. By 1830, society was instructing some 137,639 pupils in 1,621 schools.

1877: Cahir Healy, Nationalist politician and writer, born at Mountcharles, Co. Donegal.

3/12

1897: Kate O'Brien, novelist and dramatist, born in Limerick. Works include *The Land of Spices* (1941) and *That Lady* (1946).

1916: Seán Ó Ríordáin, Irish language poet, born in Ballyvourney, Co. Cork. Collections include *Eireaball Spideoige* (1952).

1976: Dr Patrick Hillery installed as sixth President of Ireland.

1982: Dr Patrick Hillery installed as President of Ireland for a second term.

1990: Mary Robinson installed as seventh President of Ireland.

4/12

1879: Sir Hamilton Harty, composer and conductor, born in Hillsborough, Co. Down.
    Became internationally famous as conductor of Halle Orchestra, Manchester, 1920–33. Self-taught composer, orchestral arranger and conductor, his arrangement of 'My Lagan Love' and his own 'Sea Wreck' remain particularly popular.

1971: In Belfast, seventeen people died when UVF bomb exploded without warning at McGurk's public house – single biggest loss of civilian life in history of post-1969 'Troubles' up to that date.

5/12

1924: Death of Edward Martyn, playwright.
    Made significant contribution to modern Irish culture. 1899, helped found Irish Literary Theatre with Lady Gregory, W.B.

Yeats and his cousin, George Moore. 1902, with help of £10,000 of own money, founded famous Palestrina choir in Pro-Cathedral, Dublin.

In later years, became virtual recluse at home in Tulira Castle, Co. Galway. Remains, which he initially left for dissection by medical students, are interred in unmarked grave in Glasnevin cemetery.

6/12

1921: Anglo–Irish Treaty was signed in London.

Under terms of the Treaty, 26 counties of Ireland established as Irish Free State with same constitutional status within British Empire as nations such as Australia and Canada. Northern Ireland recognised as separate area and provision made for a boundary commission to make changes in border between two states. Members of Free State parliament to take oath of allegiance to Crown, and Britain to retain three naval bases.

1982: In Northern Ireland, sixteen people, including eleven British soldiers, died when bomb, placed by INLA, exploded without warning at 'Droppin' Well' public house in Ballykelly, Co. Derry. Seventeenth person died later from injuries.

7/12

1688: Apprentice Boys of Derry slammed gates of city against King James' troops.

Though officially decided to admit new garrison – a Catholic regiment of Lord Antrim's Redshanks – the thirteen apprentice boys took matters into their own hands by seizing keys of gates. The 105-day Siege of Derry took place the following year, in April 1689.

8/12

1831: Death of James Hoban, architect of White House.

Born near Callan, Co. Kilkenny, emigrated to America in 1785. 1792, won competition for design for President's House, later the White House, in Washington. Corner-stone laid by George Washington in 1793. When White House destroyed by British in 1814, Hoban commissioned to rebuild it.

1856: Death of Fr Theobald Mathew, temperance campaigner.

1881: Padraic Colum, poet and dramatist, born in Longford town. Works include *The Land* (1905) and *Thomas Muskerry* (1910).

1922: Execution of 'The Provincial Martyrs'.
Four Republicans – Dick Barrett, Rory O'Connor, Joe McKelvey and Liam Mellows – executed in Mountjoy jail in retaliation for fatal shooting of Dáil deputy Seán Hales in Dublin the previous day.

9/12

1922: Irish Senate met for the first time.
Made up of sixty members, of whom thirty elected by Dáil Éireann and remainder, mainly from Protestant landlord class, nominated by President of the Executive Council. This first Senate was abolished in 1936.

1973: Sunningdale Agreement was signed.
Agreement, between Irish and British governments and Unionist, Alliance and SDLP parties in Northern Ireland proposed to establish power-sharing executive in Northern Ireland, council of Ireland and Anglo–Irish law commission.

10/12

1891: Viscount Harold Alexander, field marshal, regarded as one of finest Allied commanders in Second World War, born on family estate at Caledon, Co. Tyrone.

1977: Máiréad Corrigan and Betty Williams, co-founders of 'Peace People' in Northern Ireland, awarded 1976 Nobel Peace Prize in Oslo.

11/12

1905: Erskine Hamilton Childers, fourth President of Ireland (1973–4), born in London, son of author and patriot, Robert Erskine Childers.

1956: IRA 'border campaign' began.

Primarily aimed at destruction of property, was called off in February 1962. Claimed eighteen lives: eight IRA members, four Republican supporters and six RUC members.

1979: Charles J. Haughey elected Taoiseach by Dáil Éireann, having succeeded Jack Lynch as leader of Fianna Fáil.

12/12

1803: Gerald Griffin, dramatist, novelist and poet, born in Limerick. Works include *The Collegians* (1829).

1883: Peadar Kearney, songwriter, born in Dublin.
Wrote words of 'A Soldier's Song' at 10 Lower Dominic St, Dublin, in 1907. Music composed by his friend Patrick Heeney who died in 1911 at the age of 29 and was buried in an unmarked grave in Drumcondra churchyard. Poem was first published by Bulmer Hobson in *Irish Freedom* in 1912, and was later adopted as marching song by Irish Volunteers. 1923, 'A Soldier's Song' translated into the Irish 'Amhrán na bhFiann' by writer and civil servant Liam O'Rinn. Subsequently, though never officially or legislatively adopted, 'Amhrán na bhFiann' became accepted national anthem of 26-county state.

13/12

1867: Clerkenwell prison explosion, London.
In an unsuccessful attempt to rescue a comrade, Richard O'Sullivan Burke, a group of Fenians blew up wall of Clerkenwell prison. Twelve died and over fifty were injured.

1868: Death of Dr Henry Cooke, Presbyterian leader renowned as 'the framer of sectarianism in the politics of Ulster'.

14/12

1791: Rev. Charles Wolfe, poet, born at Blackhall, Co. Kildare. Works include 'On the Burial of Sir John Moore' (1817).

1831: Battle of Carrickshock.
At Carrickshock, Co. Kilkenny, a mob of two thousand clashed with forty policemen on 'tithe duty'. Chief constable and sixteen of his men killed and seven seriously wounded.

1918: General Election.

> Sinn Féin won 73 seats, although forty-five of their candidates in prison. Unionists won 25 seats and Irish Party reduced to 6 seats. Independent Unionists won 6 seats.

1982: Twenty-fourth Dáil Éireann assembled.

> Dr Garret FitzGerald elected Taoiseach in Fine Gael–Labour coalition government.

15/12

1963: Death of Oscar Traynor, soldier and politician.

> Brigadier of Dublin Brigade during War of Independence, led attack on Custom House in 1921. Toured Europe as goalkeeper for Belfast Celtic football club and was Minister for Defence in several Fianna Fáil governments.

1992: Death of Liam O'Leary, film historian and author, regarded as elder statesman of Irish cinema. Works include *An Invitation to Film* (1945) and *The Spirit and the Clay* (1967).

16/12

1936: Frank Ryan led Republican followers to Spain to fight in International Brigade in support of Republican government.

> Ryan's 'Connolly Column', named after Irish Socialist martyr and numbering about a hundred and fifty, served in Spain until a few months before fall of Madrid to General Franco in March 1939. More than a third of their number were never to return. A month previously – in November 1936 – General Eoin O'Duffy left Ireland with his seven-hundred-strong Irish Brigade to support Franco and his nationalist rebels. Most of his men returned after 6 months.

1967: Death of Cecil Lavery, Supreme Court judge.

1971: Death of General Richard Mulcahy, soldier and politician.

17/12

1785: Sir William Napier, general and author of classic *History of the War in the Peninsula* (6 vols, 1828–40) born at Celbridge, Co. Kildare.

1834: First railway in Ireland and world's first suburban railway, from Dublin to Kingstown (Dún Laoghaire), was opened.

1857: Death of Sir Francis Beaufort, Navan Co. Meath-born rear-admiral and hydrographer who originated scale of wind velocities named after him.

1907: Death of William Thomson Kelvin, Lord Kelvin, scientist who discovered second law of thermodynamics. Inventor of numerous instruments for measuring electricity.

18/12

1850: James Bourchier, correspondent of *The Times* in the Balkan Peninsula, born at Baggotstown, Co. Limerick.

1865: Death of Rev. Henry Montgomery, leading Presbyterian and noted Arian.

19/12

1919: During War of Independence, viceroy, Lord French, narrowly escaped assassination by IRA at Ashtown in Dublin.

1974: Cearbhall Ó Dálaigh installed as fifth President of Ireland.

20/12

1822: Dion Boucicault, dramatist, actor and man of the theatre, born in Dublin. (Some sources say 26 December 1820).

A prolific author, credited with about 150 plays, including translations and adaptations of novels, an input which prompted him to suggest that his tombstone might bear the words 'His first holiday'. Best remembered for 3 Irish plays; *The Colleen Bawn* (1860), based on Gerald Griffin's novel *The Collegians*, *Arrah na Pogue* (1864) and *The Shaughraun* (1874).

Probably the natural son of Dr Dionysius Lardner, a boarder in his mother's home.

1866: Maud Gonne MacBride, revolutionary, born in Aldershot, England, daughter of army officer of Irish descent and English mother.

1909: The 'Volta', Ireland's first cinema, opened in Mary St, Dublin, with James Joyce as manager.

1961: 26-year-old Robert McGladdery from Newry, Co. Down, became last man to be judicially executed in Ireland.

   Hanged in Crumlin Road jail, Belfast, for murder of 19-year-old Pearl Gamble, also from Newry. Last judicial execution in Republic of Ireland enacted 7 years previously.

21/12

1843: Death of Edward Bunting, musician and antiquary.

   Born in Armagh, was greatest pioneer in previously neglected field of Irish music. Collected and published some 300 different traditional tunes, many of which were taken up later and restored to popular use by poets and songwriters such as Thomas Moore.

1900: Death of Vere Foster, philanthropist and educationalist.

   Spent over 50 years and a considerable fortune working to improve social conditions in Ireland. Spent his last years working for relief of Belfast's sick-poor.

1915: Death of Violet Florence Martin, novelist under pen-name Martin Ross and literary partner of her cousin, Edith Somerville. Works include *Dan Russell the Fox* (1911) and *In Mr Knox's Country* (1915).

1977: Death of Seán Keating, landscape and figurative painter. Works include 'Men of the West' (1915), evoking romantic austerity of west of Ireland.

22/12

1916: Six hundred Irish internees released from Frongoch detention camp in Wales.

   Though fewer than two thousand actively participated in 1916 Rising, over three thousand afterwards arrested by British authorities. Of these, over a thousand released, fifteen executed, a hundred and twenty-three sentenced and deported to English prisons, while a thousand, eight hundred and sixty-three served with internment orders and sent to Frongoch.

At Frongoch, Michael Collins established his ascendancy. From his comrades in the camp, formed nucleus of his Dublin assassination 'squad' and built up many of the contacts for his countrywide intelligence organisation.

Remaining prisoners at Frongoch released under general amnesty in January 1917.

1989: Death in Paris of Samuel Beckett, writer, playwright and winner of Nobel Prize for Literature (1969).

23/12

1916: Death of James O'Kelly, war correspondent and politician.

1958: Death of Dorothy Macardle, historian. Works include *The Irish Republic* (1937).

24/12

1601: Battle of Kinsale, Co. Cork, in which forces of Hugh O'Neill and Hugh O'Donnell were defeated by Lord Mountjoy.

1823: Death of James Gandon, architect of some of Dublin's finest buildings, including the Custom House (1791), the Four Courts (1802) and the King's Inns.

1895: Death of William John Fitzpatrick, biographer. Works include *The Correspondence of Daniel O'Connell with his Life and Times* (1888).

25/12

1829: Patrick Sarsfield Gilmore, bandmaster and composer, born in Dublin. Works include 'When Johnny Comes Marching Home'.

1835: Death of Antoine Ó Reachtabhra (Raftery), Gaelic poet.

1860: An t-Athair Pádraig Ó Duinnín, editor and lexicographer, born at Carn, Rathmore, Co. Kerry.

1873: Patrick 'Paddy the Cope' Gallagher, founder of Temple-crone Co-operative Society (1906), born at Cleendra, Co. Donegal, eldest of a family of nine.

1881: Sir John Dill, field marshal and confidant of President Roosevelt and General Marshall, born in Lurgan, Co. Armagh.

26/12

1591: Escape of Red Hugh O'Donnell and Henry Art O'Neill from Dublin Castle.
Subsequently rescued in Dublin mountains by Fiach Mac-Hugh O'Byrne. O'Neill died of exposure but O'Donnell eventually reached Donegal.

1950: Death of James Stephens, poet, storyteller and novelist. Works include *The Crock of Gold* and *The Charwoman's Daughter* (1912).

27/12

1849: Death, aged 41, of James Fintan Lalor, Young Irelander and advocate of 'the land of Ireland for the people of Ireland'.

1904: Abbey Theatre opened in Dublin with double bill, *On Baile's Strand* by W.B. Yeats and *Spreading the News* by Lady Gregory.

1969: Death of Dan Breen, revolutionary and politician.
Represented Tipperary as Fianna Fáil TD for 33 years. Better remembered, however, for exploits during War of Independence (1919–21).

28/12

1787: Death of Denis O'Kelly, racehorse owner.
Owner of famous horses such as Scaramouch, Gunpowder and, notably, Eclipse. Won famous wager, 'Eclipse first and the rest nowhere' when Eclipse won Queen's Plate at Winchester.

1883: St John Greer Ervine, dramatist, novelist and critic, born in Belfast. Works include *Mixed Marriage* (1910), *Boyd's Shop* (1935) and *Robert's Wife* (1937).

1894: Death in San Francisco of James Graham Fair, miner and millionaire.
   Born near Belfast, made his fortune in Nevada silver mines. His deposits of gold and silver yielded $100 million in 6 years.

29/12

1850: Death of William Hamilton Maxwell, novelist. Works include *Wild Sports of the West of Ireland* (1832) and *Barry O'Linn* (1848).

1937: Constitution of Ireland came into operation.
   Drafted almost single-handedly by Eamon De Valera. In referendum held in July 1937 it was approved by 685,105 votes to 526,945.

30/12

1691: Death of Robert Boyle, natural philosopher, renowned for 'Boyle's Law'.

1830: Rev. William Blackley, social reformer, born in Dundalk, Co. Louth.
   Based in England, Blackley advocated compulsory national insurance and the provision of old age pensions. These were eventually introduced in 1911 and 1908 respectively. Died in 1902 before his ideas bore fruit.

31/12

1602: Donall Cam O'Sullivan, Chief of O'Sullivans of Beare, Co. Cork, set out on epic 200-mile trek from Glengariff to Ulster.
   Resolving to seek refuge in Ulster after defeat of Irish at Battle of Kinsale, Munster chieftain set out with a thousand followers – four hundred fighting men and six hundred non-combatants: women, children and elderly. When, 15 days later, eventually found sanctuary with Brian Oge O'Rourke at Leitrim Castle, party of a thousand had been reduced to just

thirty-five, including one woman. Remainder had either been killed or had fallen from starvation, exhaustion and exposure.

1909: First powered flight in Ireland.

Harry Ferguson, in monoplane powered by 8-cylinder air-cooled JAP engine, built by himself, travelled 150 yards, about 12 feet off the ground on Downshire estate at Hillsborough, Co. Down.

1962: Telefís Éireann, Republic of Ireland's first television station, went on air for the first time.

Centenaries

1994

1094: Malachy – Mael Maedoc – Saint and Archbishop of Armagh
(b.)
1494: Poyning's Law, restricting legislation in Irish parliament to
measures that had first been approved of by English
Council, was passed.
1594: Trinity College, Dublin opened (9 Jan.)
Irish College founded at Douai
Ware, Sir James, antiquary and historian (b. Dublin, 26 Nov.)
1694: Hutcheson, Francis, philosopher (b. Co. Down, 8 Aug.)
MacCarthy, Justin, Viscount Mountcashel (d. 21 July)
1794: Brocas, William, portrait painter (b. Dublin)
Carleton, William, novelist (b. Clogher, Co. Tyrone, 4 Mar.)
Gill, Michael Henry, master printer (b. Co. Offaly)
Haverty, Joseph Patrick, portrait and subject painter
(b. Galway)
Hely-Hutchinson, John, politician and provost of TCD
(d. 4 Sept.)
Maclear, Sir Thomas, astronomer (b. Newtownstewart,
Co. Tyrone, 17 Mar)
Moran, Michael, balladeer known as 'Zozimus' (b. Dublin)
O'Connor, Feargus, Chartist leader (b. Connorville, Co. Cork,
18 July)
Robinson, Richard, C of I Archbishop of Armagh, Primate and
founder of Armagh Observatory (d. 10 Oct.)
Woodward, Richard, C of I Bishop of Cloyne (d. 12 May)
1894: In rugby, Ireland achieved her first Triple Crown win
(Belfast *v* Wales, 10 Mar.)
The Irish Agricultural Organisation Society was founded by
Horace Plunkett (18 Apr.)
Irish Trades Union Congress (ITUC) met for the first time
(27–8 Apr.)
Thirty-eight Achill Islanders drowned en route to Scotland
(14 June)
Beach, Thomas Miller, alias Henri Le Caron, spy, (d. 1 Apr.)
Conway, Edward Joseph, biochemist (b. Nenagh,
Co. Tipperary, 3 July)
Daunt, William Joseph O'Neill, Repealer and Home Ruler
(d. 29 June)

Fair, James Graham, miner and millionaire (d. 28 Dec.)
Heron, Archie, socialist and trade union organiser,
    (b. Portadown, Co. Armagh)
Hone, Evie, artist (b. Co. Dublin, 22 Apr.)
Ireland, Denis, author and Irish senator (b. Belfast)
Lavery, Cecil, supreme court judge (b. Armagh, 6 Oct.)
Lynam, William Francis, soldier and writer (d.)
McMaster, Anew, actor (b. Monaghan)
Saul, Captain Patrick J, aviator (b. Dublin)
Smyllie, Robert Marie, journalist (b. Glasgow)
Starkie, Walter Fitzgerald, author (b. 9 Aug.)
Tierney, Michael, president of UCD (b. Ballymacward,
    Co. Galway, 30 Sept.)
Tuohy, Patrick, painter (b. Dublin)
Waller, John Francis, author (d. 19 Jan.)

***

1995

1295: Ireland was divided into counties
    Massacre of the O'Connors of Offaly (Dec. 25)
1595: Battle of Clontibret, Co. Monaghan; victory for Hugh O'Neill,
    Earl of Tyrone over Sir Henry Bagenal (13 June)
    Fitzgerald, Walter Reagh (executed 10 Mar.)
    Garvey, John, C of I Archbishop of Armagh (d. 2 Mar.)
1695: Parliament passes penal laws (7 Sept.)
    O'Hempsey, Denis, harper (b. Garvagh, Co. Derry)
1795: Lord Lieutenant Fitzwilliam dismissed (23 Feb.)
    United Irishmen reconstituted as a secret, oath-bound society
      (10 May)
    'Battle of the Diamond', Loughgall – first Orange Lodge
      formed (21 Sept.)
    St Patrick's College, Maynooth, formally opened (1 Oct.)
    Callanan, Jeremiah John (J.J.), poet (b. Cork)
    Darley, George, poet and mathematician (b. Dublin)
    Jackson, Rev. William, United Irishman (d. 30 Apr.)
    King, Edward, Viscount Kingsborough, author (b. Cork,
      10 Nov.)
    Ó Súilliobháin, Tadhg Gaedhealach, poet (d. 22 Apr.)
    Whitty, Michael, journalist (b. Enniscorthy, Co. Wexford)
1895: Manslaughter of Brigid Cleary – the 'Tipperary Witchcraft
    Case' (15 Mar.)

Oscar Wilde sentenced to two years imprisonment for homo-
sexual offences (25 May)

Fifteen members of Kingstown (Dún Laoghaire) lifeboat
drowned (24 Dec.)

Alexander, Mrs Cecilia Frances, hymn-writer (d. 12 Oct.)

Fitzpatrick, William John, biographer (d. 24 Dec.)

Lane, Denny, Young Irelander and poet (d. 29 Nov.)

Lenihan, Maurice, journalist and historian (d. 25 Dec.)

McQuaid, John Charles, Archbishop of Dublin (b. Cootehill,
Co. Cavan, 28 July)

O'Gorman, Richard, Young Irelander (d. 1 Mar.)

Reddin, Kenneth, district justice and author (b. Dublin)

Shaw, William, provisional leader of Home Rule Party
(1879–80) (d. 19 Sept.)

***

1996

1696: Porter, Sir Charles, Lord Chancellor (d. 8 Dec.)

1796: First Orange Order 'Twelfth' demonstration (12 July)

Kilmainham Gaol, Dublin, received its first inmates (12 Aug.)

First sitting at new Four Courts, Dublin (3 Nov.)

Admiral Hoche's expedition to Ireland – broken up by storms
(22–9 Dec.)

Banim, Michael, writer (b. Kilkenny, 5 Aug.)

Crozier, Francis Rawdon, explorer (b. Banbridge, Co. Down)

Graves, Robert James, physician (b. Dublin)

Kennedy, John Pitt, engineer and agriculturalist, (b. Carn-
donagh, Co. Donegal, 8 May)

O'Curry, Eugene, scholar (b. Carrigaholt, Co. Clare)

Quain, Jones, anatomist (b. Co. Cork)

1896: Limavady or Broighter gold hoard was discovered (Feb.)

John Dillon elected leader of anti-Parnellites (18 Feb.)

First screening of a cinema film in Ireland, using the Lumière
process, took place in Dublin (20 Apr.)

'Irish Socialist Republican Party' was founded by James
Connolly (29 May)

Balfour's Land Act was passed by parliament (14 Aug.)

Irish Race Convention was held in Dublin (1–3 Sept.)

Cheyney, Peter, pen-name of Reginald Evelyn Peter Southouse-
Cheyney, writer (b. Co. Clare, 22 Feb.)

Clarke, Austin, poet, dramatist and novelist (b. Dublin, 9 May)
Fleming, John, scholar (d. 28 Jan.)
Higgins, Frederick Robert, author (b. Foxford, Co. Mayo,
    24 Apr.)
O'Connor, Michael P, broadcaster and writer (b. Loughrea,
    Co. Galway)
O'Donovan, Harry, comedy scriptwriter (b. Dublin)
O'Flaherty, Liam, writer (b. 24 Aug.)
Shields, Arthur, actor (b. Dublin)
Tuke, James Hack, Quaker philanthropist (d. 13 Jan.)
Wilde, Lady Jane Francesca, pen-name 'Speranza', writer
    (d. 3 Feb.)

***

1997

597: St Colmcille of Iona (d. 9 June)
1597: Gunpowder explosion at Winetavern St, Dublin – hundred and
        twenty-six killed (11 Mar.)
      O'Byrne, Fiach MacHugh, chief of O'Byrnes of Wicklow
        (murdered 8 May)
1697: Joy, Francis, printer and papermaker (b. Belfast)
      Macklin, Charles, actor and dramatist (b. *c.* 1697,
        d. 11 July 1797)
1797: Burke, Edmund, political writer and orator (d. 9 July)
      Hamilton, William, diviner and naturalist (murdered 2 Mar)
      Hughes, Most Rev. John, first archbishop of New York, 1850
        (b. Annaloghlan, Co. Tyrone, 24 June)
      Kendrick, Matthew, marine painter (b. Dublin)
      Lover, Samuel, novelist and painter (b. Dublin)
      Orr, William, United Irishman (executed 14 Oct.)
      Power, William Grattan Tyrone, actor (b. Kilmacthomas,
        Co. Waterford 2 Nov.)
1897: Oireachtas – Irish Literary Festival – first held (17 May)
      Dracula by Bram Stoker, published
      Archer, William, naturalist and librarian (d. 14 Aug.)
      Haughton, Samuel, scientist (d. 31 Oct.)
      Jellet, Mainie, artist (b. Dublin)
      Kiernan, Thomas J, diplomatist and author (b. Dublin)
      O'Brien, Kate, novelist and dramatist (b. Limerick, 3 Dec.)
      Ó Caoimh, Pádraig, general secretary of GAA 1929–64
        (b. Roscommon)

Ó Deirg, Tomás, politician (b. Westport, Co. Mayo, 26 Nov.)

***

1998

1598: The Battle of the Yellow Ford (Co. Tyrone, 14 Aug.)
1698: Connor, Bernard, medical doctor (d.)
Molyneux, William, philosopher and patriot (d. 11 Oct.)
Ó Bruadair, Dáibhidh, poet (d.)
Wogan, Sir Charles, Jacobite soldier of fortune (b. *c*)
1798: Arrest of Lord Edward FitzGerald (19 May)
Rising in Leinster began (23 May)
Battle of Oulart Hill (27 May)
Battle of New Ross (4 June)
Battle of Antrim (7 June)
Battle of Arklow (9 June)
Battle of Ballynahinch (13 June)
Battle of Vinegar Hill (21 June)
Battle of Ballinamuck (8 Sept.)
Banim, John, writer (b. Kilkenny, 3 Apr.)
Cooper, Edward, astronomer (b. Dublin)
Croker, Thomas, antiquary (b. Cork, 15 Jan.)
Guinness, Sir Benjamin, brewer (b. Dublin, 1 Nov.)
Holwell, John, survivor of 'Black Hole of Calcutta' (d. 5 Nov.)
Long, John St John, painter and quack (b. Co. Limerick)
MacDonnell, Alexander, chess player (b. Belfast)
McCracken, Henry Joy, United Irishman (executed 17 July)
Madden, Richard, historian of the United Irishmen (b. Dublin, 20 Aug.)
Reid, Rev. James, church historian (b. Lurgan, Co. Armagh)
Scott, John, Earl of Clonmel, chief justice (d. 23 May)
Tone, Theobald Wolfe, United Irishman (d. 19 Nov.)
1898: First Gaelic League *Feis* at Macroom, Co. Cork (20 Mar.)
De Valois, Ninette, founder of Sadler's Wells Ballet School (b. Co. Wicklow, 6 June)
Fitzmaurice, Col. James C, aviator (b. Dublin, 6 Jan.)
Gallagher, Frank, journalist (b. Cork)
Gilbert, Sir John, historian (d. 23 May)
Lewis, Clive, novelist and critic (b. Belfast)
Lynch, Patricia, children's writer (b. Cork)
O'Malley, Ernest, writer and Republican (b. Co. Mayo)
Quain, Sir Richard, physician (d. 13 Mar.)

1999

1599: 'Pass of the Plumes', Timahoe, Co. Laois – Owney O'More
    defeats Lord Lieutenant Essex (17 May)
    Lynch, Rev. John, historian (b. Galway)

1699: Malone, Molly, Dublin fishmonger (buried, 13 June)
    Pearce, Sir Edward Lovett, architect (b. Co. Meath)

1799: Black, Dr Joseph, physician (d. 26 Nov.)
    Callan, Nicholas, priest, scientist, inventor (b. Dromiskin,
    Co. Louth, 20 Dec.)
    Caulfield, James, first Earl of Charlemont (d. 4 Aug.)
    Costello, Louisa, miniaturist and writer (b.)
    Dargan, William, railway contractor (b. Carlow, 28 Feb.)
    Kilmaine, Charles Jennings, general in French army (d. 15 Dec.)

1899: First issue of *An Claidheamh Soluis* organ of the Gaelic League
    (18 Mar.)
    Catholic Truth Society of Ireland founded (20 June)
    Publication of *Some Experiences of an Irish RM* (Somerville and
    Ross)
    Armstrong, Sir Alexander, naval surgeon and explorer
    (d. 4 July)
    Barry, Gerard, piper (d. 6 Apr.)
    Bowen, Elizabeth, novelist (b. Dublin, 7 June)
    Carberry, Hugh, Armagh Nationalist (d. Boer War, 30 Oct.)
    Carty, Francis, author (b. Wexford)
    Cusack, Margaret Anne, the 'Nun of Kenmare' (d. 5 June)
    Deane, Sir Thomas Newenham, architect (d. 8 Nov.)
    Grant, Albert, company promoter (d. 30 Aug.)
    Graves, Charles, C of I bishop and mathematician (d. 17 July)
    Hogan, Michael, the Bard of Thomond (d.)
    Lemass, Seán, Taoiseach (1959–66) (b. Ballybrack, Co. Dublin,
    15 July)
    MacLíammóir, Micheál, actor, writer, man of the theatre,
    (b. Cork, 25 Oct.)
    Macardle, Dorothy, historian (b. Dundalk, Co. Louth)
    Ó Buachalla, Liam, scholar (b. Dublin)
    O'Dea, Jimmy, comedian (b. Dublin)
    O'Growney, Fr Eugene, Irish language revivalist (d. 18 Oct.)
    Ó Lochain, Micheál, Irish language revivalist (d. 10 Jan.)
    Starkie, Enid, critic (b. Dublin)

***

2000

1600: Battle of Moyry Pass, Co. Armagh (2 Oct.)
   MacMahon, Heber, bishop and general (b. Farney,
      Co. Monaghan)
   O'Malley, Grace, sea captain (d.)
1700: Pilkington, Rev. Matthew, lexicographer (b. Ballyboy,
      Co. Offaly)
1800: Daniel O'Connell made his first public speech (13 Jan.)
   Irish Parliament opened for its last session (15 Jan)
   First ordination to priesthood at St Patrick's College, Maynooth
      (6 June)
   Act of Union received royal assent (1 Aug.)
   Butler, John, Lord Dunboyne (d. 7 May)
   Connellan, Owen, scholar (b. Co. Sligo)
   Grubb, Thomas, optician (b. Kilkenny)
   Hall, Anna Maria, author (b. Dublin, 6 Jan.)
   Hennessy, Richard, soldier and distiller (d.)
   Hogan, John, sculptor, (b. Tallow, Co. Waterford, 14 Oct.)
   Mahon, Charles James Patrick, the O'Gorman Mahon,
      politician and soldier (b. Ennis, Co. Clare, 17 Mar.)
   Ní Chonaill, Eibhlín Dhubh, who wrote lament, 'Caoineadh
      Airt Uí Laoghaire' (d.)
   Parsons, William, third Earl of Rosse, astronomer (b. York,
      17 June)
   Rothwell, Richard, painter (b. Athlone, 20 Nov.)
   Smithson, Harriet Constance, 'Madame Berlioz' (b. Ennis, Co.
      Clare, 18 Mar.)
   Whaley, Thomas 'Buck' or 'Jerusalem', adventurer (d.)
1900: Queen Victoria in Ireland (4–25 Apr.)
   Burton, Sir Frederick, painter (d. 16 Mar.)
   Carroll, Paul, playwright (b. Blackrock, Co. Louth, 10 July)
   Collis, William, doctor and author (b. Dublin)
   D'Alton, Louis, playwright and theatrical producer (b.)
   Dillon, Myles, celtic scholar (b. Dublin)
   Foster, Vere, philanthropist (d. 21 Dec.)
   Guthrie, Sir Tyrone, theatre producer (b. Kent)
   Kernoff, Aaron or Harry, artist (b. London, 9 Jan.)
   Larminie, William, civil servant and writer (d. 19 Jan.)
   Mulhall, Michael, statistician, (d. 13 Dec.)
   Norton, William, labour leader (b. Dublin)
   O'Faolain, Seán (b.)
   O'Flanagan, James, author, (d.)

Rowsome, Leo, piper, (b. Co. Wexford)
Russell, Charles, Baron Russell of Killowen, Lord Chief Justice
of England (d. 10 Aug.)
Wilde, Oscar, wit and dramatist (d. 30 Nov.)

***

2001

1601: The Battle of Kinsale, Co. Cork (24 Dec.)
1701: King James II (d. 16 Sept.)
1801: Act of Union came into force (1 Jan.)
Benn, George, historian of Belfast (b. 1 Jan.)
Kennedy, Patrick, author (b. Co. Wexford)
Newman, John Henry, Cardinal, theologian (b. London,
21 Feb.)
O'Higgins, Ambrose, viceroy of Peru (d. 18 Mar.)
Parnell, Sir John, Chancellor of Irish Exchequer (d. 5 Dec.)
1901: Bracken, Brendan, publisher and politician (b. Templemore,
Co. Tipperary)
Fitzgerald, George, natural philosopher (d.)
Henn, Thomas, Yeatsian scholar (b. Sligo)
Johnston, Denis, actor and dramatist (b. 18 June)
Lawlor, John, sculptor (d.)
Luby, Thomas Clarke, Fenian (d. 1 Dec.)
Rooney, William, poet (d. 6 May)
Stephens, James, chief founder of the Fenians (d. 29 Apr.)

***

2002

1602: Donall Cam O'Sullivan Beare marched to Leitrim with a
thousand followers (31 Dec.–3 Jan.)
Collins, Donagh, Jesuit (hanged, 31 Oct.)
O'Donnell, Red Hugh (d. 31 Aug.)
1702: Nugent, Robert, Earl Nugent, politician and poet
(b. Carlanstown, Co. Westmeath)
William III, King, formerly Prince of Orange (d. 8 Mar.)
1802: Barter, Richard, physician (b. Cooldaniel, Co. Cork)
Burke, Aedanus, American revolutionary statesman
(d. 30 Mar.)

Dermody, Thomas, poet (d. 15 July)

Fitzgibbon, John, Earl of Clare, Lord Chancellor (d. 28 Jan.)

Higgins, Francis, The 'Sham Squire' (d. 19 Jan.)

Lytton, Lady Rosina, novelist (b. Co. Limerick, 4 Nov.)

O'Leary, Fr Arthur, author (d. 8 Jan.)

Patterson, Robert, naturalist (b. Belfast, 18 Apr.)

Thomas, George, the 'Rajah from Tipperary' (d. 22 Aug.)

Wall, Joseph, Governor of Goree (executed, 28 Jan.)

1902: Barry, Kevin, medical student and IRA Volunteer (b. Dublin, 20 Jan.)

Blackley, William, cleric and social reformer (d. 25 July)

Croke, Dr Thomas, RC Archbishop of Cashel and Emly (d. 22 July)

De Vere, Aubrey, poet, (d. 21 Jan.)

Gorham, Maurice, journalist and author (b. London)

Hayes, Richard, librarian and bibliographer (b. Abbeyfeale, Co. Limerick)

Hector, Annie, novelist under name Mrs Alexander (d. 10 July)

Killen, Rev. William, historian (d. 10 Jan.)

Pakenham, Edward, Earl of Longford, theatrical producer and dramatist (b. 29 Dec.)

Ryan, Frank, Republican and socialist (b. Elton, Co. Limerick)

***

2003

1603: Treaty of Mellifont (30 Mar.)

MacEgan, Owen, vicar apostolic of Ross (slain, 5 Jan.)

1703: Brooke, Henry, poet, dramatist and novelist (b.)

1803: Robert Emmet's Rising in Thomas Street, Dublin (23 July)

Barry, John, commodore in United States navy (d. 13 Sept.)

Coyne, Joseph Stirling, playwright (b. Birr, Co. Offaly)

Cullen, Cardinal Paul (b. Prospect, Co. Kildare, 29 Apr.)

Despard, Edward, conspirator (hanged, 21 Feb.)

Emmet, Robert (hanged, 20 Sept.)

Fitzgibbon, Edward, angler and writer (b. Limerick)

Griffin, Gerald, dramatist, novelist and poet (b. Limerick, 12 Dec.)

Guinness, Arthur, founder of Guinness' Brewery (d. 23 Jan.)

Hervey, Frederick Augustus, fourth Earl of Bristol (d. 8 July)

Hussey, Thomas, bishop and first president of St Patrick's College, Maynooth (d. 11 July)

La Touche, William, banker (d. 7 Nov.)
Malton, James, architectural draughtsman (d.)
Mangan, James Clarence, poet (b. Dublin, 1 May)
Neilson, Samuel, United Irishman, (d. 29 Aug.)
O'Brien, William Smith, Nationalist (b. Co. Clare, 17 Oct.)
Russell, Thomas, United Irishman (executed, 21 Oct.)
Tandy, James Napper, revolutionary (d. 24 Aug.)
Thornton, Matthew, signatory of American Declaration of
    Independence (d. 24 June)
Woulfe, Peter, chemist (d.)
1903: Blackburn, Helen, pioneer suffragette (d. 11 Jan.)
Bradley, Bishop Denis Mary, youngest United States bishop in
    1884 (d. 13 Dec.)
Close, Maxwell, Irish revivalist (d. 12 Sept.)
Deevy, Teresa, playwright (b. Waterford)
Duffy, Sir Charles Gavan, Nationalist (d. 9 Feb.)
Lecky, William, historian (d. 22 Oct.)
O'Connor, Frank, writer (b. Cork, 17 Sept.)
O'Meara, Robert, professor of medicine (b. Bruff, Co. Limerick)
Osborne, Walter, painter (d. 24 Apr.)
Stokes, Sir George, mathematician and physicist (d. 1 Feb.)

***

Bibliography

Boylan, Henry, *A Dictionary of Irish Biography*, Gill and Macmillan, Dublin 1978
Doherty, J.E. and Hickey, D.J., *A Chronology of Irish History since 1500*, Gill and Macmillan, Dublin 1989
Webb, Alfred, *A Compendium of Irish Biography*, Gill, Dublin, 1878, Unabridged Republished Edition, Lemma Publishing Corporation, New York, 1970

Bardon, Jonathan, *A History of Ulster*, Blackstaff Press, Belfast, 1992
Beckett, J.C., *The Making of Modern Ireland 1603–1923*, Faber, London, 1966
Hough, G.L., *Dictionary of Dates*, Chambers, Edinburgh, 1983
McMahon, Seán (ed.), *A Book of Irish Quotations*, O'Brien Press, Dublin 1984
Montague, H. Patrick, *The Saints and Martyrs of Ireland*, Colin Smythe Ltd, Buckinghamshire, 1981
Lyons, F.S.L., *Ireland Since the Famine*, Fontana, London, 1971
Wallace, Martin, *100 Irish Lives*, David and Charles, London, 1983

Irish News, The, Belfast
Irish Press, Dublin
Irish Times, The, Dublin

General Index

Index of Names

Index of Place Names

(Author's note: As Dublin City occurs on almost every date, only County Dublin is included here. Entries outside Ireland comprise countries and 3 cities – London, New York, Moscow)